Katherine Dunham lay on the floor of the hut with the other voodoo initiates. As she joined in a dance to the gods, where shoulders moved spasmodically forward and then jerked back rhythmically, she felt an overwhelming ecstasy. Dance was why she had come to Haiti and dance helped her to understand the traditions of that country. Shaken and exhausted by the three-day-long voodoo ceremony, Katherine Dunham acknowledged that the time spent in Haiti was crucial to her personal and professional development—a turning point in her life.

Repressed by an overly-strict father, subjected to racial prejudice as a young girl, Katherine Dunham grows into a complex, determined, and accomplished black woman. Her interest in dance goes back to early childhood when she watched cousins in vaudeville shows and later organized a cabaret at the age of fourteen.

Katherine Dunham's anthropological studies, beginning with the West Indies trip, inspired her to give black dance the attention it deserved. She soon opened her own school and later formed the Katherine Dunham Dance Company. The troupe received tremendous critical acclaim as it performed a new kind of dance incorporating the African tradition. And throughout their world travels, Katherine carried the heavy burden of keeping a touring company financially and emotionally intact.

The dances that Katherine Dunham choreographed are still performed by such noted dance groups as the Alvin Ailey Dance Company in New York. Terry Harnan's original research and personal interviews make this a unique and revealing book about a woman who has become a classic figure in her own time.

African Rhythm
American Dance

A BIOGRAPHY OF
Katherine Dunham

BY TERRY HARNAN

Alfred A. Knopf ✕ *New York*

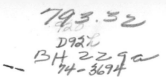

Grateful acknowledgment is made to the following for permission to reprint copyrighted material:

Doubleday and Company, *Island Possessed*, Katherine Dunham, © 1969; Harcourt, Brace & World, Inc., *A Touch of Innocence*, Katherine Dunham, © 1959; Harcourt, Brace & World, Inc., *Sunset and Twilight*, Bernard Berenson, © 1963; Henry Holt & Co., Inc., *Journey to Accompong*, Katherine Dunham, © 1946, now available from Greenwood Press, Westport, Connecticut.

Grateful acknowledgment is made for the use of illustrations:

The Katherine Dunham Papers, Southern Illinois University at Carbondale, ii, 107, 108, 109, 110, 111, 112, 113, 114, 115; Katherine Dunham Private Collection, 116.

Library of Congress Cataloging in Publication Data

Harnan, Terry. African rhythm—American dance.
  SUMMARY: A biography of the black dancer and choreographer noted for her dances drawn from African and Caribbean sources.
    1. Dunham, Katherine—Juvenile literature.
[1. Dunham, Katherine. 2. Dancers] I. Title.
GV1785.D82H37 1974 793.3'2'0924 [B] [92] 73-15113
ISBN 0-394-82644-2 ISBN 0-394-92644-7 (lib. bdg.)
Manufactured in the United States of America

Acknowledgments

I wish first to thank Katherine Dunham, currently Director of the Performing Arts Training Center and Dynamic Museum at East St. Louis for the chance to interview her in person during a busy season, and for giving me permission to examine her papers, deposited in the University Archives of Southern Illinois University at Carbondale. For assembling books and papers for my inspection, and for other courtesies rendered during my visit to the Performing Arts Center I want also to thank Jeanelle Stovall and other members of Katherine Dunham's staff.

My deep gratitude goes to Kenneth Duckett, Curator of the Special Collection at Southern Illinois

University, Carbondale, and Assistant Curator David Koch for their kindness and patient help in getting up box after box of the Katherine Dunham papers at my request, and for making the facilities and comforts of the Rare Book Room available for my research.

My warm appreciation also to Mrs. Frances Dunham Catlett, widow of Albert Millard Dunham Jr., whose memories of her husband and generous reminiscences of the years in Chicago were invaluable. Thanks also are due to Dr. Eugene Clay Holmes, retired Professor of Philosophy from Howard University, who contributed information about Albert Dunham's academic career.

For library assistance beyond the call of duty, I want to record my thanks to Mrs. Alice Wells, formerly head of the Southold Free Library and now retired, who expanded local resources through the cooperation of the New York State Library Extension Service, particularly in obtaining xeroxed copies of magazine articles. Other essential library service and biographical information was rendered by the staff of the Library and Museum of Performing Arts in New York City, especially Curator Genevieve Oswald.

Last but not least I am grateful to Virginia Bennett Moore for serving as a sympathetic sounding board during the writing of the book and for making many helpful comments and suggestions during the reading and proofreading of the manuscript.

Contents

III Ventures Into the Unknown

IV Some Endings and New Beginnings

African Rhythm—American Dance

Background and Beginnings

1

The Curtain Goes Up

The time was 1946, the place New York, but inside the darkened Belasco Theatre the audience was transported to the West Indian island of Martinique, witnessing practices and beliefs that blacks had brought over with them from Africa. The Dunham Dance Company was performing *L'Ag'Ya*, the story of how Julot, a vengeful, rejected suitor of the girl, Loulouse, obtained magic help from the King of Zombies to win her away from her true beloved.

Playing the part of Loulouse was the American dancer, beautiful, brown-skinned Katherine Dunham. Resisting Julot's powerful love fetish at first, she then danced Loulouse's gradual helpless surrender to its power. Only the appearance of her fiancé, Alcide, broke the Voodoo spell, as he challenged Julot to the Ag'Ya, the Martinique fighting dance for which the dance-drama was named. Though Alcide won the contest, evil triumphed as the frustrated Julot stabbed him in the back. Loulouse was left to grieve alone over the body of her slain lover as the curtain came down.

Visibly moved by the performance they had just seen, the audience clapped through several curtain calls. The vibrant, dark-eyed Katherine Dunham was applauded not only for her role as Loulouse, but for planning the narrative and choreographing the dances of the entire drama of *L'Ag'Ya*. Program notes told playgoers of her long stay, years before, among the peoples of the Caribbean. Still, newspaper reporters had further questions to ask when they swarmed backstage for interviews. They found her sitting at her dressing table, exhausted but happy at the success of her show. Her lithe dancer's body was covered by a loose man's white shirt to protect her costume as she removed her makeup.

"Miss Dunham, what is the inspiration for *L'Ag'Ya?*" one reporter asked.

Her voice was pleasantly low and soft as she answered, "In the fishing village of Vauclin, in Martinique, the Ag'Ya is danced on feast days. I used it as a theme for a story I invented for the stage."

"Is the Ag'Ya danced to resolve courtship rivalry there?"

"It is not necessarily a dance of courtship rivalry at all." She went on to explain how she believed the Ag'Ya originated in the Nigerian spring festival in Africa. Men held wrestling matches to honor the Earth Mother and make her proud of her sons. But they know such testing of men's strengths might threaten the authority of the West Indian plantation owner who'd imported them as slaves to work his sugar cane fields. So the Africans ritualized the wrestling match into a dance and that way it became acceptable; the threat was removed.

"What about the Zombie scene, Miss Dunham?"

"The inspiration for that also came from Africa, via the West Indies. There I heard many stories about sorcery used to raise people from the dead to become slaves, called Zombies."

"Is it true you were initiated into Voodoo?"

She nodded slightly, knowing the next question would probably be, "How much did you believe in it?" She had no intention of answering that so she went on to talk of other things more directly related to the show. This was neither the time nor place, she thought, to explain her complicated feelings about Voodoo ritual—to tell about her own confusions and discomforts, and her sense of fulfillment at the end of the initiation when she danced.

Her interest in dance was what first led her to the West Indies. As a young student of anthropology she was eager to find evidences of black culture—especially the dance—that had traveled from Africa on slave ships to the new world. Over and beyond her scholarly interests, Katherine felt that her acceptance by the blacks of the Caribbean as one of them, her sharing of their daily life and activities, was more enriching spiritually and emotionally than anything that had happened to her before. She found sources of inspiration that would last the rest of her creative life, to help her through all the struggle, heartbreak, and occasional despair to come. Dance was the bright thread that connected all the experiences of Katherine Dunham's life.

2

A Richly Varied Childhood

Katherine Dunham was three years old when she first felt the urge to dance on the stage. Her Uncle Arthur Dunham, a voice coach and choral leader, was directing a musical drama titled *Minnehaha* that he and other theatrically aspiring Dunhams hoped to produce. Aunt Clara Dunham and her daughter Irene had provided the initiative and played leading roles. Rehearsals were held in the basement of the tenement where Katherine and her older brother Albert lived with their Aunt Lulu Dunham. Left alone in the upstairs apartment, Katherine wandered to the basement where she came upon people wearing feathers and war paint, doing an American Indian war dance. Immediately she started to join in the fun but her Aunt Clara said she was too young to take part and ordered her upstairs.

Minnehaha opened at Chicago's Monogram Theatre in 1913. Though it lasted only a few nights, the number of Dunham participants gave clear evidence that theatre was in Katherine's blood—along with African, Madagascan, Canadian-French, and American Indian blood. Born on June 22, 1909 in Glen Ellyn, Illinois, the baby named Katherine Dunham was a small League of Nations—largely black.

Katherine's mother was dead by the time Katherine discovered those basement rehearsals. Fanny June Taylor, later Dunham, had first married a Russian Jewish man with whom she had five children before he died. She then married Albert Dunham, who was many years younger than she was, and became the mother of Albert Jr. and Katherine. Building a house in Glen Ellyn, near Chicago, the new family enjoyed several happy years together before Fanny became fatally ill. Though Katherine was still very young when her mother died she always remembered how Fanny looked, her hair shining in the lamplight, playing musical duets with Katherine's father on Sunday evenings.

Broken-hearted at losing his wife, Albert Dunham took a traveling job selling suiting goods. He left his children with their Aunt Lulu who lived in Chicago's crowded, poverty-stricken South Side. Albert, who was four years older than his sister, spent his days at school. But when Aunt Lulu left to work as a beautician in her clients' homes there was a question about what to do with little Katherine.

For a while a stage-struck second cousin solved that problem by taking Katherine with her to afternoon vaudeville shows. At Chicago's Grand Theatre or the Monogram, four-year-old Katherine saw and heard future stars of Broadway musical revues—Buck and Bubbles, Cole and Johnson, Ethel Waters, and Bessie Smith. Sometimes, overcome by the smoke-filled air, she fell asleep on her cousin's lap to be pinched awake when it was time to go home.

"Now remember, don't you tell," her cousin would warn.

To pay for their theatre tickets the cousin filched money that Aunt Lulu left for buying coal and food. After their escapades they had to rush back to the one-room flat before Aunt Lulu got home, in order to start a small fire in the grate, attempting to make it look as if a fire had been burning all day.

Toddling through the streets holding her cousin's hand, Katherine would pass other children dancing at the corners for pennies, a blind man playing a violin, some drunks fighting, and derelicts snoring in littered doorways. As they neared home they might see the blue cart of the hot tamale man painted with its red and yellow hearts and hear the cheery steam whistle that made Katherine's mouth water.

"Tamaleh, Tamaa——leh! Come and get 'em while they're hot. Hot tamaa-leh!" he sang out.

Tamales would often be on the supper table along

with the sweet rolls or cream pastries Aunt Lulu would bring home with her as treats.

Another treat was their Sunday visits to see music coach Uncle Arthur at Mecca Flats, the four-story tenement where he lived. Leaning over the gallery railing that surrounded the central courtyard, Katherine and Albert were fascinated by the real life dramas going on all around them. Doors banged as people walked or soft-shoed from one flat to another. The court echoed with bursts of music from phonograph records of Ma Rainey shouting the blues or risqué witticisms of Bert Williams. Mixed with the wailing of babies were snatches of dialogue from loving or quarreling men, women, and children. Below them the cement courtyard was covered with broken bottles and spilled garbage. Above, laundry flapped in the wind on the roof.

These remembrances enriched Katherine Dunham's development as an artist and a human being. But her mother's relatives did not consider it a fit life for growing children.

The way in which the children lived was discovered by a half-sister, one of the more light-skinned children from Fanny June Taylor's first marriage. This younger Fanny, now with a family of her own, came visiting one wintry afternoon to see how young Katherine and Albert were getting along at Aunt Lulu's flat.

She found the children sniffling with colds, huddled in blankets before a coal stove whose fire was dying out. Further investigation disclosed that the bathroom, located in the outside hall, badly needed cleaning. So did the community kitchen where Fanny Weir could find no food in the pantry labeled Dunham. She came back grimly to order the children, "Get your things together."

Albert objected. He didn't want to leave, at least not until Aunt Lulu got home, but Fanny Weir insisted. Bundling the children and their few belongings into a cab, she brought them to her own home. In Fanny Weir's comfortable steam-heated apartment there was plenty of hot, nourishing food served at regular times. The children were taught to bathe daily in their own bathroom and went to bed early. All this greatly benefited their physical well-being, but there were drawbacks.

Fanny Weir's children, who had always been snobbish about their light skin color, teased Katherine and Albert for their darker color and tightly curled hair. So Katherine's first experience with racial prejudice ironically was at home, at the hands of her own family.

When Aunt Lulu and their father, Albert Dunham Sr., tried to regain possession of the children a court decision upheld Fanny Weir's action. Aunt Lulu had to go out as a visiting beautician only because she had been denied renewal of the lease for her small beauty shop. She did not have a comfortable home to offer the children because she was poor. It was only because Albert Sr. was a traveling salesman that he was away for such long periods. But to the court all this looked like "neglect" and "desertion." Katherine unknowingly made matters worse when she truthfully described her visits to vaudeville houses and various other incidents in her Aunt Lulu's household.

Katherine was confused, and when she caught her brother's disapproving look she felt guilty without knowing why. Aunt Lulu bowed her head and cried. Katherine's father was called before the bench to be told he must prove to the judge's satisfaction that he could take proper care of his children before they would be restored to his charge. It was the first time, Katherine later said, that she learned honesty does not in itself guarantee justice.

Katherine was five years old and her brother nine before their father was granted custody of them. By then he had saved up enough money to buy a dry cleaning shop in the town of Joliet, Illinois, forty miles from Chicago, where they would make their new home. Accompanying him was a small, slim woman with high cheekbones and warm brown eyes.

"This is your new mother," he said, introducing Annette Poindexter, a former schoolteacher from Iowa who had become his second wife. So the children got a home and a full set of parents at the same time.

But this big man the children so strongly resembled—the same round face and dark eyes and chocolate brown skin and tight, curly hair—was like a stranger to them. They remembered a more youthful man, affectionate and happy, playing musical duets with their mother in the parlor of their first home in Glen Ellyn. This stern face didn't seem to belong to the father who'd once held them on his knees and told tales about Br'er Rabbit to comfort them during their mother's illness.

Actually they knew very little about their father. Katherine recalled a story about him she had heard her elders tell many times. It was an incident that took place about a year before she was born. The Dunham's property in Glen Ellyn had been bought through Albert's light-skinned wife. When the neighbors found out that the black man accompanying her was not an employee but her husband they set off a bomb that smashed a window in the house then under construction. It was meant as a warning to leave town. Instead of taking flight, Albert Dunham took up residence in the tool shed armed with a double-barrelled shotgun, and stayed there every night until the house was finished. No further damage was done.

Courage, then, was one of their father's characteristics. The children were soon to learn about others. Meanwhile their life in Joliet began pleasantly. A horse named Lady Fern was bought to haul the clothes delivery van. On Sunday mornings, the family often piled into a surrey with a fringed top, and Lady Fern decorously pulled them to the nearby countryside. They picnicked on the grass, and while the grownups napped, the children explored the woods or waded in the running brook trying to catch fish. On other Sundays, Katherine and her father would take Lady Fern out and race her, keeping those trips secret from Annette, who would have surely disapproved.

These happy outings grew fewer as Albert Dunham's fierce determination and driving ambition became more evident. Something had changed Albert Dunham since the children's early memories of him. His deep grief over his first wife's death turned to bitterness as he helplessly watched Fanny June's holdings being sold to cover debts incurred by the children of her former marriage. Even their Glen Ellyn home, which held such happy memories for him, eventually went under the auctioneer's hammer.

Resolved to build his own estate, in defiance of his wife's relatives, Albert Dunham pushed hard at everyone, always demanding much of himself and those around him. As his drive towards accomplishment increased, his affection for others seemed to wither. Working so hard, he gradually forgot how to relax or enjoy times with his family.

Everyone was expected to play a part in the father's schemes for the future. Annette ran the household, kept the store's account books, and did the mending and clothing alterations. Young Albert picked up and delivered customers' clothes and was otherwise kept so busy he had to cut his sleeping hours short to get his homework done. Katherine tagged the clothes and helped Annette in the house.

But Katherine was still too young to get caught up as her brother was in the increasing number of chores. She started going to the ivy-covered Beale School and made good marks in music, reading, writing, cooking, and sewing—and especially in physical education. Bodily activity gave her great joy. It was a release for all the tensions built up at home.

However Katherine wasn't very good at science, didn't like arithmetic, and got bad conduct marks for whispering to friends in class. These friends belonged to a secret society organized and led by Katherine in response to her feeling of exclusion from other groups.

Their symbol of fraternity was the Eagle Eye, an emblem ten-year-old Katherine came across in a book on American Indians that her brother had given her for Christmas. With scraps of red satin Katherine made headbands for the group. On them she sewed beads in the shape of an eye. They produced a startling effect, the eye seeming to stare from the center of the girls' foreheads. This attracted much attention, which gave the girls a lot of satisfaction but in the end led to an official school order to stop wearing the bands. While they lasted, the Eagle Eye bands gave Katherine and the others a much needed sense of belonging.

Katherine worked hard at school trying to keep up with her brother's good example and high marks. Albert was a hard act to follow, as her Uncle Arthur Dunham might say. But Katherine was not jealous of his success. The tie between brother and sister was unusually close. Deprived of both their parents' presence in their early years the children had come to depend on one another. As the elder, Albert had always been protective of Katherine. He had helped guide her first steps and patiently tried to answer her endless questions about the world around her. Throughout her childhood and into young womanhood Katherine continued to count heavily on Albert's support and advice. But inevitably there were times when Albert was so busy at store and school work that she couldn't get to talk to him. Crawling into bed one night Katherine noticed a bright star, shining as if framed in her high bedroom window. She watched it until she fell asleep. The next night at the same time she saw the star there again. Soon she began looking for it the minute she turned out her light.

She was fascinated by the fact that the star was so far away, seeming so pure and untouched by the struggles of her everyday life. This made her feel safe to confide in it, to tell it of her triumphs and confusions, fears and failings. She began talking to the star and made up a prayer. "Help me star. Help me. Make me strong, give me courage, make me know the right thing to do." Without the help of any formal church training Katherine had found her own religion. Meanwhile there was another influence at work.

Though distantly separated from Chicago's stage

shows and Uncle Arthur Dunham and Mecca Flats, Katherine found another tie to theatrical life in Joliet. An old vaudevillean named Mrs. Jameson lived at the top of the cliff in back of the Dunham dry cleaning shop. Katherine visited her often.

This was an adventurous outing from beginning to end. Stepping from rock to rock up the steep hill, Katherine would come to an iron fence that surrounded a school playground at the hill's crest. Holding tightly to the iron bars she would inch her way along until she came to the overgrown backyard of a dilapidated old mansion.

The large, red brick house looked almost sinister with shutters closing its tall upstairs windows like eyes that had been blinded. But the handsomely panelled front door made Katherine feel welcome. The lady who lived behind it was always glad to see Katherine. She was a gray-haired, pale, and wrinkled woman named Mrs. Jameson and she had once been "in the theatre."

Invited to come in for tea, Katherine couldn't help noticing the musty smell of the place. To conserve heat and save housework the old woman used only three rooms, downstairs, and seldom opened the windows. The rest of the house, including all the upstairs rooms, was shut off.

Heavy pieces of furniture stuffed with horsehair stood around the living room. The floor lamps had fringed, beaded shades. In the corner were several trunks covered with old leather and studded with brass nails. These trunks were full of mementoes from Mrs. Jameson's theatrical past. After tea the old lady would open them and take out their endless treasures of costumes, shoes, feathers, paste jewelry, and scarves. Katherine was allowed to handle these, to try them on herself, and even to take a few things home with her to keep.

There were also old pictures and newspaper clippings telling about Mrs. Jameson's theatrical career. The photos showed a rather plump and smooth-skinned young woman wearing long white tights and high-laced shoes. Hours flew by as Katherine and the old woman chatted together.

For a while these talks gave the only hint of what Katherine's future career was to be. As she grew older she entertained many ambitions. When she got a nurse's kit Katherine devoted herself to taking care of wounded animals—cats, mice, birds. Her stepmother declared she'd grow up to be a doctor. But then Katherine mixed up beet roots with cold cream to make rouge and dreamed of becoming a cosmetician like her stepmother's brother, Uncle Ed Poindexter. Later she said she wanted to be an explorer and go to Africa.

The trouble was that all the explorers anyone had heard of or read about up to that time were men. So the question remained—what would Katherine grow up to be?

3

Troubled Adolescence

Katherine entered high school the same year that her brother began junior college. The high school was a larger building than the Beale or Farragut grade schools, packed with more students than she had ever seen in the lower grades. Confused by this system of going to a different classroom for each subject, she was afraid that she would get lost in the maze of hallways.

But as she became better acquainted with the geography of the school, with fellow students and teachers, her fears gradually subsided. "Miss Dunham" was how thirteen-year-old Katherine was now addressed in flattering recognition of her growing maturity. She liked the more adult challenges that high school life presented, the greater freedom to select more of the subjects she liked and to develop her own particular interests.

Music remained one of her favorite subjects and she yearned to belong to a high school group called the Terpsichorean Club, named after the ancient Greek muse of choral song and dancing. To qualify for membership she joined a dancing class and was taught to run around the big gymnasium, waving her arms gracefully in the air to the rhythm of a thumping tom-tom or gong. She also practiced how to sit, stretch, jump, and fall without hurting herself.

Her reward for doing well in these classes was to take part in the school's annual dance recital the following spring. With other beginners Katherine leaped about as a wood nymph trailing a scarf, and posed as a tree with outstretched arms. Between these first brief stage appearances she stood in the wings to watch the more expert solo performers.

One soloist in particular excited her envy and admiration. The girl wore a spectacular bright red high-necked costume with white boots. Springing into the air she twirled into a spirited Russian dance. Towards the end, going into a squatting position with folded arms, the girl danced the Hopak, thrusting first one leg out and then the other in an example of magnificent body control. People throughout the auditorium murmured praise of this feat to one another before bursting into applause.

Katherine decided she must learn to do the Russian dance to win such approval from an audience herself someday. She worked hard at her dancing. Membership in the Terpsichorean Club became one of her important goals.

School-related activities, however, could not take up all her time. She had to help out at her father's shop which was now doing more business than ever. Albert Dunham had added carpet cleaning to the regular clothes cleaning service. He had bought an expensive piece of equipment, which the children called the dust wheel, that mechanically beat the dirt out of very large and heavy rugs.

Though his pride in this machine was enormous, the rest of the Dunham family regarded it with mixed feelings. They were grateful for the extra money the dust wheel brought in. It paid for electricity in the shop and their upstairs apartment in place of kerosene and gas lamps. It also made possible some new clothes, occasional summer vacations, and music lessons. But they couldn't help resenting the longer hours they all had to put in at the shop. Annette suffered headaches and muscle cramps from fatigue. The children were robbed of time needed for school work and play.

Worst of all was when the dust wheel broke down, which often seemed to happen at mealtime. The machine's subterranean rumbling, though not a pleasant background to dinner table conversation, was to be infinitely preferred to the silence that followed a breakdown.

Albert Sr., listening to the silence for a moment, would impatiently throw down his napkin. "Come along," he'd say, beckoning to his son.

This was what Katherine dreaded. She would get up and follow them, uninvited, to the huge room in the other half of the building that housed the dust wheel. First her father would use a plank to prop up the wheel. This created a narrow opening through which young Albert had to squeeze, dropping into the dark pit below where the dust gathered.

It was Albert's task to locate the broken strap that had caused the wheel to stop, and to splice it. Katherine wondered how anyone could be sure the machine wouldn't suddenly start going again while her brother was down there. She knew her brother wondered about that too.

Because of her loving concern for him, Katherine watched her brother closely enough to see the sweat break out on his trembling upper lip and the fierce frown he put on to hide his terror from his father. She knew how he had to brace himself each time in order to face this terrible task. She wouldn't leave until her brother returned. She felt her presence and her prayers helped protect him until he came up out of the darkness.

The family knew that much of Albert Dunham's pride in the dust wheel was based on the fact that no one else in their community could have afforded to buy it. Through his ownership of the wheel, despite its occasional breakdowns, Albert Dunham proved himself to be a successful businessman. That was the judgment of the community, and he basked in it. Many visitors sought and valued his opinions on local and national political events as well as business matters.

Albert Dunham was convinced that the road in life he had taken was the only one to follow, and he had little patience with other points of view. He was not impressed that his son had been elected president of his senior class and then named class valedictorian. Or that Katherine had written a class poem and a story which were accepted and published in *Child Life* Magazine.

"I have two wonderful children," Annette told the neighbors who offered their congratulations.

"What kind of future will it get them?" their father wondered skeptically.

He held the firm belief that only if a man owned his own business did he become somebody. Albert Dunham could buy anything he wanted, he declared. So when Katherine was told she needed private lessons to learn the Russian dance, which was not taught at school, she asked her father to pay for them. To her great joy, he consented, nudged by Annette. Then, as if to further impress upon his family the tangible results of running your own business, he drove up to the shop one afternoon in a handsome second-hand Studebaker he'd just purchased.

Neighbors came flocking to take a look. Automobiles were scarce at that time, in the early 1920's, and people were impressed by this shiny black open touring car with a folding canvas top and leather upholstery. This was quite a step up from the battered delivery wagon that had preceded it.

Albert had learned to drive in order to deliver clothes to the store's customers, and now he was enlisted to teach Katherine to drive. She could hardly believe her ears. Her father, it seemed, wanted someone other than himself to take Annette to her various church functions. Whatever the motive, Katherine was delighted to learn to handle the sporty new car.

She soon became adept at driving, benefitting from her brother's warning, "Remember, Kitty, if you ever have an accident he'll never let you drive again. So just don't have one!"

The automobile opened up another world for the Dunham family as it did for so many others. In the summer of 1921 Katherine and her stepmother took off with a friend to visit Annette's relatives in Alton, Illinois. Along the way they planned to stop at Chouteau Street in St. Louis, a black social mecca, to try the famous fried fish.

When they reached Chouteau Street Katherine leaned out the car window and gaped openly at the sights. She saw women with dresses cut low to bare their shoulders to the cool river breezes. The women wore finger rings and necklaces of big, glass beads. Many men's shirts were casually open at the throat and others sported diamond stickpins in colorful silk scarfs. They spoke in soft voices with southern dialects and threw back their heads to laugh easily and often. Here Katherine first heard the blues, as she listened to the music out of every doorway. In the guttering candlelight of the dark rooms beyond, Katherine saw shining wet faces lifted in song or bowed lovingly over guitars. She noticed that men and women showed their affection for one another quite openly.

Such natural display and gaiety appealed to her. She remembered Mecca Flats as having something of this spirit but on a grimmer, more sordid scale. Chouteau Street had style, and she was charmed by it. She thought the fried fish sandwich she ate was the most delicious food she'd ever tasted. In later years she likened it to the first ritualized sacrificial food taken in dedication to a new way of life.

Back in Joliet the memory of Chouteau Street gave Katherine the impetus she needed to stand up one night in Brown's African Methodist Episcopal Church with a bold new idea. The church was considering how to raise money for a new parish house. There were the usual suggestions about holding a church supper or a cake sale. Katherine found herself on her feet, heart pounding, as she said "I would like to organize a cabaret party."

What Katherine knew about cabarets she had heard second-hand from her mother's more sophisticated, light-skinned relatives in Chicago. They often went to cabarets and had talked about them in front of Katherine. People sat at little round tables eating and drinking while they watched different kinds of entertainment. It would give Katherine the opportunity she wanted to perform the long-practiced Russian dance.

A few church members were shocked by the idea but most of them nodded indulgently. Surely a fourteen-year-old girl's ideas of a café couldn't be very wicked. The project was approved and Katherine put in charge. She named it the Blue Moon Café.

Katherine recalled all the talks she'd had with Mrs. Jameson on the cliff, the Chicago vaudeville acts she had seen, and movies she had gone to since then. Drawing on all these sources for inspiration, Katherine went to work.

She wrote verses for a Mistress of Ceremonies, chose songs and singers, and decided on the dances to be performed. She planned to take a chief role in most of these activities. This time she wasn't going to be satisfied with the small part she'd played at the school's annual dance recital.

Sympathizing with her stepdaughter's feelings, Annette offered to sew the costumes. Katherine was surprised to hear her father say, "I'll see if I can't get the Brotherhood of Elks to rent us their hall." When he returned with the news that the Elks had agreed, Albert Dunham went further and volunteered to be a soloist at the café. He wanted to sing his favorite number, "Asleep in the Deep." Katherine concluded that the theatrical urge must be very strong in the Dunham family.

All went well until the morning of the performance when Katherine woke up with a sore throat and high fever. She was too full of nervous excitement to sleep well for many nights and had run herself down. A few hours later Katherine lost her voice and burst into tears.

This meant all her speaking and singing parts must be taken by others, but Katherine stubbornly insisted on going to the Blue Moon Café. By gestures she indicated to the family doctor that she could still dance. He gave her some medicine and reluctantly granted permission.

Every seat in the house had been sold out for the Blue Moon Café. Peeking through the curtains at the large audience Katherine was seized with stage fright. It would be the first time she had ever performed a solo dance before the public. Stumbling onstage she began an oriental number she called "Anitra's Dance," her limbs stiff with terror. Every slight misstep made her blush furiously at her own awkwardness. She was so relieved to exit at the end that she hardly heard the applause.

But later she did the Russian dance so well that, by popular demand, she had to repeat the Hopak until she almost fainted from her exertions. Bouquets of flowers were brought onto the stage. Then she went home to bed.

The Blue Moon Café was a financial success. Even selling tickets at the low price of twenty-five cents each they had cleared a profit of seventy-six dollars and everyone was pleased. Further, they all agreed that Katherine had been the hit of the show.

4

Struggling Young Womanhood

*I*n the cold, trying months of the winter ahead the Blue Moon Café was a warm memory. Katherine had to take over more household responsibilities so that her stepmother could help with the heavier load of work that was coming into the shop. With less free time than ever at her disposal she had to cut down on her dancing lessons and skip hockey and basketball games though she longed to make the school team. Yet she managed well enough to be invited into the Girls' Athletic League, and she won a mark of 99 on her Latin test.

Albert, under rigorous training and pressure to succeed his father as head of the business, had a harder time of it. A brilliant scholar, he wanted to go on to a university to study philosophy, and to teach. There were increasing family quarrels about this and other matters as Annette tried to get her husband to ease up on the demands he made on all of them. Far from being the wicked stepmother of the fairy tales, Annette was a hard-working, loving woman, though not given to open demonstrations of affection. The children knew they had an ally in her.

But she was unable to soften Albert Dunham's bitter opposition to his son's scholastic aspirations. Once, when Albert was studying at night, his father ran downstairs and deliberately shut off the electricity, then gloated over his triumph. But there was no deprivation or beating that could make young Albert swerve from the life course he had chosen. Katherine marveled that her brother was so incorruptibly sure of what he wanted to be and do. At least in school he got the recognition he deserved.

Then came an unexpected blow. In junior college Albert was again nominated for class president, a position he'd held before in his high school career. But this time a white boy got up to protest—on the grounds that Albert was black. While Albert listened in horror and embarrassment, he heard himself and the black race both attacked and defended by his white classmates.

It was an astonishing, dismaying experience. Annette Dunham blamed the incident on the northward migrating flood of blacks who, by their sheer numbers, were causing problems in housing and employment. White people resented this more and more.

Now, under no circumstances would young Albert, deeply hurt by the turn of events, agree to continue as a candidate for class president. He withdrew his name from nomination and neither his classmates, nor Annette, nor Katherine could persuade him to change his mind.

However Annette did not mean to take this kind of treatment without protest. After Katherine complained that her music teacher made the class sing songs portraying blacks as weak, idle, and brainless people Annette scheduled an interview with the school principal. She carried with her a petition signed by many prominent townsmen—good customers of the shop—objecting to such songs. As a result, the principal ordered the songs discontinued and the music teacher was transferred to band instruction. Annette also got the name of Albert Dunham Jr. restored to the honor role in the school lobby after someone tried to blot it out.

Only in a small town like Joliet, Albert told his sister, could things like this happen. He wanted to leave to enter a big city university and had already applied for a scholarship to the University of Chicago. He asked Katherine to keep this news a secret.

Katherine couldn't imagine life without her brother's daily, comforting presence. When word came that Albert was granted his scholarship, to start at the beginning of the next academic year, she broke down and wept. But Albert assured her that she could come to the university too when she was ready. Katherine sobbed that she didn't think she'd ever be able to win a scholarship as Albert had.

"You've got to think about getting away, that's all," Albert said. "Don't give up, Kitty. Don't ever give up. You'll make it all right!"

Meanwhile quarrels at home intensified. Business at the store was not as good as it had been and this worried Katherine's father. He thought up a new scheme, hoarding his money to speculate in real estate. He became so miserly that Annette didn't have enough to manage the household or replace the children's worn-out shoes. During their quarrels Albert began hitting his wife, once breaking her glasses. Protesting such mistreatment, Annette left home. The children missed her terribly. Finally, receiving assurances from her husband that he would act differently in the future, she was persuaded to return. For a while everything was better, but then the tension started to build up again.

Affairs came to a head one February night when Albert Dunham struck his son for practicing the cello. Young Albert, tried beyond endurance, hit back for the first time. The two men fought, rolling on the floor and knocking over furniture. A muscular young worker from the shop downstairs had to be called to separate them.

In a voice choked with emotion, Albert Dunham then ordered his son to leave home and never to come back again. His young son stared back at him defiantly. Annette pleaded with both of them, wringing her hands: "Albert, he's your *father*—oh Al, *don't don't*, he's your son! Al, Al, you don't know what you're saying."

Young Albert turned on her: "He's no father of mine. And don't ever say it again!" Without waiting for his supper, not knowing where he would go, Albert tied his few belongings in a cardboard box. He was so blind with fury he didn't even look at Katherine as he gathered a load of books under his other arm and clattered downstairs and out of the house.

Not long after, Annette left home again too. This time Katherine begged to go with her. They rented part of a small house in another section of town. Yet the bonds with husband and father were not completely severed. Albert Dunham took his wife alterations and mending to do at her new home. Katherine still was required to put in hours of work at the shop after school.

In this way Katherine and her stepmother earned the money to get along. They sent young Albert food and whatever extra money they could scrape together. He was in Chicago by then. His scholarship took care of his tuition and books, but he had to find work to pay for his meals and lodging. He was having a hard time. Albert Sr. did not respond to appeals made by Katherine and her stepmother that he help his son.

"He is no son of mine, and if he thinks he's big

enough to strike his father, he is certainly big enough to make his own way," said Albert Dunham unforgivingly.

Katherine thrived in the greater freedom of life away from her father. She achieved the long-sought membership in the Terpsichorean Club, won the center position on the girls' basketball team, and was elected president of the Girls' Athletic Association. Still she had little of the social life other girls enjoyed. Her father had laid down the law that she was not to go out with boys and Annette supported him. In answer to Katherine's protests about this, Annette kept repeating, "After all, he's your father."

After Katherine graduated from high school the situation remained the same. There was only one social affair in Joliet that her father approved of. This was the annual Christmas Charity Ball which the Dunhams still attended as a family group. Though Albert Dunham insisted he have all the waltzes with his daughter, he allowed a very few chosen young men to take her for the other dances. Wearing one of the new gowns Annette specially sewed for her, Katherine was thrilled whenever an escort led her onto the polished ballroom floor to the strains of the latest musical hit.

She might not have known the latest steps if it hadn't been for Albert. During Katherine's first year at junior college her brother was given a full fellowship at the University of Chicago, with more financial security than he'd ever known before. He was even able to save enough money to come home occasionally for weekends to visit his sister and stepmother in Joliet.

He brought college friends with him who, by teaching Katherine songs and dances that were popular in Chicago, gave her a taste of the good times other teenage girls were having. Though the Charleston was by then outmoded, the Slow Drag and Mooch were coming in. Katherine learned fast.

Katherine's father also allowed her to attend a few parties given in Chicago by her mother's relatives. Now and then Albert accompanied his sister to these affairs but they bored him. Katherine was not very happy either. Tall for her age—five feet seven—she felt awkward and out of place, having little in common with anyone there. Talking about sports, or books she'd read, she was miserably aware that the city boys preferred the light-hearted nonsensical talk they exchanged with the other girls. It was ironic that Katherine, who loved dancing and did it so well, spent a great deal of her adolescent party time as a wallflower.

So disheartening were these experiences that she started to question her dream of joining Albert in going to the University of Chicago. She wasn't at all sure how well she'd make out in city life. Now in her last year of junior college she'd soon have to make up her mind.

One morning there was a letter from her brother enclosing an application for a part-time library job in Chicago. Katherine wasn't too quick about filling it out. Finally she sat down to list her academic references and answer the questions. She was eighteen years old. She described her hair as dark brown with a streak of auburn in it. She had brown eyes. Team sports were prominent among her extracurricular activities.

Soon another letter followed setting a date for an examination she must take in Chicago. Only after she had taken and passed the examination did she realize that the part-time library job was due to start several weeks before her junior college graduation.

Katherine wondered if she could really break away—leave Joliet and everything familiar to her since childhood. There was another reason she might want to stay. Among her school friends was a boy who refused to be discouraged by her father's habitual disapproval. New to town, William Booker was his name. Like Katherine, he was an accomplished athlete. He gave his basketball letter to Katherine but she was made to hand it back. She wasn't able, either, to accept his invitations to school dances or other social events.

Still Bill Booker stayed around to spend whatever time with her that he could. If her father didn't call for her in the delivery wagon, Bill was able to walk Katherine to the dry cleaning shop.

That year an important basketball game was being played to decide the state school championship. Bill had two tickets and he wanted Katherine to go with him. She said her father would never consent. On his own initiative Bill Booker decided to ask Mr. Dunham directly for his permission.

The result was that Albert Dunham, in a towering rage, came pounding on Annette's door. Demanding to see Katherine he made many unjust accusations about the kind of girl she'd turned out to be. Katherine was at first speechless. But when her father struck her, it was as if a dam were opened, spilling a torrent of words in which she expressed all her resentment against him.

"This is the last time. The last time that he will ever touch me. The very last time!"

She packed her bags that night. The next morning she left for Chicago, to seek entrance to the university. With her part-time library job assured, and with her brother's help, Katherine now felt ready to make her own way. In sympathetic understanding, the school authorities mailed Katherine her junior college diploma.

II Opening of a Career

5

Life in Chicago

Katherine was no stranger to Chicago. It was where her early childhood had been spent, and she had visited relatives there in later years. But this time there were so many new experiences awaiting her that she felt like a country girl making her first trip to the city. New to her was the freedom to move about with her own age group, exploring whatever was of interest to her, and having a little money in her pocket, which she herself had earned.

The library where Katherine was to work was in an exclusive suburban section of Chicago near Hamilton Park. As Katherine gave her name to the chief librarian when she reported for her first day of work, she noticed a look of surprise on the woman's face. It occurred to Katherine that perhaps the librarian had expected someone older. Other library workers seemed so busy they barely had time to nod to Katherine during introductions. But the work was easy to do. She quickly caught on about how to use the ink pads, date stamps, and file cards.

Sitting at the front desk while the others held a conference, Katherine was soon entering and discharging books under the watchful stares of the patrons. Stiff with nervous tension because she wanted to do well, she felt that everyone else's stiffness was because she was a stranger to them. In time this would pass. They would get acquainted with each other, Katherine thought, the same way she had always made new friends each time she had to enroll in a different school.

But she was disappointed to see that the work schedule had been altered since her arrival that morning, so that no one shared her lunch hour. Returning from lunch she was shepherded into a back room. From then on her duties would be to catalog books in this room, she was told. She easily learned to do that work, too.

Not until she took the long trolley ride home did Katherine finally get a chance to think things over. Then she realized that what had happened that day had nothing to do with her being a new girl, but was because she was black. Of course they couldn't have known that until she turned up for work. This explained the chief librarian's startled look of surprise, the quick change of lunch hours, the assignment to the back room. Katherine had passed their test with high marks so they couldn't turn her away. Maybe they didn't really want to hurt her feelings either. So they simply isolated her.

That evening Albert calmly analyzed the situation. He pointed out that Katherine needed the job and it was easy, pleasant work. Though the hours would be long, added to her hours of university courses, the salary would help Katherine pay for her room and board, college tuition, and dancing lessons. The answer to this segregation was not to quit, but to stay at the job and prove to be a blameless worker.

By now, Albert was well established in the intellectual and social life at the University of Chicago. His endeavors had won him the honorary Phi Beta Kappa key in his senior year. Katherine appreciated Albert's fraternal guidance, but it presented some difficulties, too. She didn't feel she had the scholarly attitude or temperament to follow in her brother's academic footsteps. Dancing, still her chief interest, was not offered as a major at the university, and at this point she had no idea what she would select.

Meanwhile there was much to learn outside the classroom. With her brother or his friends Katherine began going to the Dill Pickle Club where she first heard lectures on what were then new and daring subjects, like birth control, trial marriage, and existentialism.

There was also the Cube Theatre, founded by Albert and some college friends, to be "an independent venture of students and artists interested in all forms of modern art." It was racially integrated, and Katherine quickly found out that if she was not acceptable to the people in the showcase library near Hamilton Park, she was cordially received by many others, especially those in the arts.

On the Cube stage Katherine played her first acting role in a dramatization of an F. Scott Fitzgerald story, "The Man Who Died at Twelve O'Clock." She met such celebrities of the day as actor Canada Lee, writer Ben Hecht, and composer W. C. Handy. They came as guest stars appearing on the Cube stage, or as patrons of its shows. With other lively, creative people—black and white—Katherine took part in stimulating discussions about the stream-of-consciousness writing of James Joyce, surrealism, and jazz.

Katherine became especially friendly with a fellow student who also enjoyed Cube Theatre activities. Frances Taylor, from Hartford, Connecticut, was a bright, pretty young black woman who had done so well in high school that she won a four year scholarship to any college she wanted to attend. The University of Chicago became her choice because a married sister living near there offered Frances the hospitality of her home. Mrs. Wilfred Ball also welcomed Frances' friends so cordially that her home developed into a social center for student gatherings.

Albert was a frequent visitor, and Katherine became Frances' roommate.

The two girls did many things together. Besides acting at the Cube Theatre they took tap-dancing lessons for a while. Then they enrolled for ballet classes with a White Russian named Ludmila Speranzeva. Trained in ballet since her childhood, Madame Speranzeva originally came to the United States with the Chauve Souris company. This popular revue differed from ballet in that it put strong emphasis on acting and story-line development in addition to dancing skills. It was to prove an important influence in Katherine's dancing career.

Unhappy with her part-time library job, Katherine wished she could teach dancing for a living. But first she must solve some major problems—getting a studio in which she could hold classes, and attracting enough students to make it pay. She wasn't quite sure how to overcome these obstacles. She envied her brother who always seemed to know how to put his thoughts into action.

Brilliant without conceit, Albert always had a more clear-sighted, steady vision of his goals. He graduated with honors and stayed to do post-graduate work at the University of Chicago, while applying for a Rockefeller grant to study under philosopher Alfred North Whitehead at Harvard. With such foundation aid he would not need an outside job, and could concentrate on getting his doctorate in Philosophy.

Albert was mature for his twenty-two years, calm and poised, but never condescending, and with a good sense of humor; qualities that made him a natural leader. Slim and attractive, with a mellow voice and laugh, he was admired and liked by everybody.

Frances Taylor was one of the girls Albert took out. Sometimes, however, he would become so involved in studying or in the creative writing he also did, that he would arrive late or even fail to show up. Albert's work always came first. He was a young man in a hurry who declared he must accomplish a lot before he was thirty, because by that time he expected to be dead. He said he would never marry.

But to Frances Taylor these drastic statements seemed the romantic posturings of youth. She was in love with Albert, but too reserved to broadcast her feelings about it. Her own family life had been a happy, loving one, and she expected and wanted the same for herself. It may have been because Frances' home experiences were so different from his own that Albert was drawn to her. When Albert's scholarship actually came through and his future seemed secure, he suddenly reversed himself and asked Frances Taylor to be his wife. Katherine was understandably stunned.

The wedding took place on Friday, the 13th of September, 1929 at the university chapel. In the wedding picture taken for the newspapers at the time Albert looks handsome and composed, his bride beamingly contented. Mrs. Wilfred Ball, Frances' sister, seems quietly pleased, and Katherine looks

proud and smiling. In fact she must have been devastated to lose her closest friend and her brother at the
same time. For her there would be many adjustments
to make.

Albert and Frances were off to live in Cambridge,
where he would attend Harvard and she would finish
college at Boston University. Katherine was left on
her own when she did not feel quite ready for that
independence.

The Wall Street crash of October 29th, 1929,
throwing the country into years of poverty called
the Great Depression, had a bracing effect on Katherine. She found herself in the company of millions
of others who were also struggling to get along. Often
she had to satisfy a ravenous appetite with half a
sandwich, or with bread and gravy. She "went hun-
gry a lot," she said. Her tuition at the university was
taken care of by a student loan. When baby-sitting
or library work didn't earn enough to pay food and
rent she borrowed from her brother. She also began
to teach dancing.

Through Cube Theatre associations Katherine had
met two leading ballet dancers from the Chicago
Opera Company. Impressed by Katherine's personality and talent, they offered to help her establish a
dance school of her own. Ruth Page advanced
twenty dollars monthly rent on a studio where Katherine could hold her classes, until such time as she
could carry it on her own. Mark Turbyfill volunteered to be one of the teachers.

Katherine had been taken to see the Ballet Russe

by her teacher, Ludmila Speranzeva. The skill and special style of its Russian dancers had brought this dance company world-wide fame. Talking it over, Mark and Katherine agreed that the special style of black people deserved to be equally well known. To call attention to this fact they decided to name Katherine's group of student-performers the Ballet Negre. While Mark would help train her students it was Katherine who must compose their dances and plan the patterns of group movement on stage. So she began working seriously at choreography, an art she was to develop into an important, life-long skill.

The annual Chicago Beaux Arts Ball, welcoming all new talent, would make an excellent showcase for the Ballet Negre to perform in without the expense of hiring a hall. It was also an ideal way to make Katherine's work better known and perhaps attract financial backing to support her school.

In 1931 Katherine's dancers put on "Negro Rhapsody" as the first act at the Chicago Beaux Arts Ball and received hearty applause from the audience. But so many of the following acts were equally well received that Katherine began to wonder whether their work had really been singled out enough for the special notice she wanted. The sensation of the evening proved to be a woman riding naked across the stage on a white horse, playing the historic role of Lady Godiva. The woman's name was Sally Rand and she later went on to a successful nightclub career. Katherine felt the evening to be a great disappointment.

For all their hard work and high hopes Katherine's students, too, felt terribly let down. Many of them began dropping out. Ruth Page and Mark Turbyfill, having done what they could for the moment, had to turn their attentions back to their own careers. In one way or another friends seemed to be falling by the wayside. Swamped by the deepening Depression, the Cube crowd's brave schemes for bold living were replaced by bitter political discussions in which Katherine did not want to take part.

During this period she married a fellow dancer named Jordis McCoo, partly to assuage her loneliness. She soon discovered that her own ambitious, high-spirited nature was not yet ready to settle down. As it happened, the marriage did not prove too demanding. Her young husband spent his nights working at the post office. In the daytime Katherine went to school and looked for an inexpensive place to rent for a studio so she could teach dancing again.

She was joined in this venture by a friend, Ruth Attaway, who taught drama. Together they shared an old stable that, though infested by bugs, had the large open spaces needed for their classes and for gatherings of people interested in the arts. It was like the old Cube Theatre days, entertaining such distinguished guests as painters Charles Sebree and Charles White, writers Langston Hughes, Sterling North, and Arno Bontemps, educator Horace Mann Bond, and others.

But when winter began they found that the studio

was too large to heat. A concerned friend, trying to be helpful, plugged the stable into the street gas main for a free ride. This worked until a policeman came one afternoon to ask a few questions. Katherine managed to talk the gas company out of prosecuting her, but they refused to deliver any more gas to the stable or anywhere else Katherine might open a studio for a while.

Until she could decide on the next course of action Katherine had to give up teaching. Everything seemed to be going wrong.

"You need, perhaps, older students," suggested Katherine's teacher, Ludmila Speranzeva, when Katherine asked her advice. Older students did not move so restlessly from place to place, Madame Speranzeva pointed out. Also many were better able to pay because they earned their own money. And it was possible that the teaching of modern dance might attract a greater number of students.

Katherine asked for her help. Ludmila Speranzeva agreed to take part in Katherine's new school, to be renamed the Negro Dance Group. The greatest contribution Madame Speranzeva made was to generously open her own studio for use by Katherine and her classes, and to coach Katherine privately in ballet and mime.

It was under Ludmila's tutelage that Katherine was first introduced to the Isadora Duncan Dance Company and Fokine. She went backstage to meet Ludmila's friend, the famous Spanish dancer, Argentina, and her partner Escudero.

Katherine already knew one of Argentina's former dancing partners, a man named Quill Munro who then lived in Chicago and occasionally visited the Cube Theatre. As a guest in Munro's apartment, Katherine had enjoyed listening to his large collection of records, petting his Siamese cats, and poring over pictures showing him as a slender, younger man in the years he'd triumphantly danced his way through Europe. Argentina gave the shyly worshipful Katherine her castanets. Quill Munro gave her the dream of someday touring Europe with her own dance company.

That was a bright hope for the future. In the difficult present Katherine was having trouble with her new dance school despite Ludmila's help. Black parents didn't want to send their daughters because they thought the name, Negro Dance Group, meant their daughters would be taught ancestral African dancing. What they wanted the girls to learn was ballet for grace and prestige, and the kind of social dancing that would prepare them for the parties and balls of their day.

Katherine was aware that many popular dance steps such as the Lindy Hop, the Cake Walk, and Black Bottom had their origins in African tribal dancing—but she couldn't go into that with the parents. Oddly enough it was a white man, Dr. Robert Redfield, who had introduced this idea to Katherine.

Pure chance had led Katherine one afternoon into Dr. Redfield's class in ethnology, a division of the Department of Anthropology at the University of

Chicago. His remarkable presentation of his material —a study of the racial, tribal, and cultural characteristics of a people—first called Katherine's attention to the remnants of African dance that still survived in the New World. He showed that people carry the stamp of their unique cultural heritage with them, across many miles and from generation to generation. This was an illumination to Katherine and fired her with the idea of tracing the roots of black dance as far as she could.

Such a study would earn her a degree in anthropology. But more importantly, it might enable Katherine to show that there was a sound black dance tradition, deserving the same respect as the white European tradition then dominating the dance stage. She had found her college major.

However, the mothers of her dance students understood nothing of this and complained that she worked their daughters much too hard. They said this would "kill their natural talent." Such statements made Katherine angry.

"That's a fallacy we've been given by the white man," she said.

Katherine recognized the fact that many blacks had innate talent as performers and artists—but that was all anyone expected of them and she felt it was not enough. Blacks could do a lot better if they put more effort and technical training into their art. Katherine believed that to ask anything less from blacks was a way of looking down on them. And she resented that.

By these convictions, Katherine showed how fast she was growing as an artist. Her own long hours of rehearsal had proved to her how much practice was needed to develop dancing skills. What looked effortless on stage was the result of months of training until muscles stopped aching to allow her to perform with grace and power.

If Katherine's words often fell on deaf ears as far as her students' mothers were concerned, the professional world of dance heard and saluted her. Her friend Ruth Page had composed a ballet titled *La Guiablesse*, a story based on Martinique folklore about a devil woman who lured men to their death, and she asked Katherine to dance in it. Katherine's husband performed the part of one of the men so fatally attracted.

When this ballet was put on at the Chicago Opera House, Katherine's father and stepmother traveled from Joliet to see their daughter dance the lead role. Having suffered years of loneliness after separation from his wife and children, the senior Albert Dunham had also undergone business reversals during the Depression. These experiences had made him look deeper into himself and perhaps helped him to better understand the part he had played in his family's alienation. He had mellowed enough over the years so that Annette was persuaded to live with him again. In the report they made to the Joliet newspaper after they returned home, the reconciled parents said they had "never enjoyed anything so much before" as seeing Katherine dance in *La Guiablesse*.

Parental pride in both children was well justified. The University of Chicago had accepted Albert Jr.'s credits from Harvard, awarding him his doctorate in philosophy, and he was teaching at Howard University in Washington, D.C. A first grandchild had arrived when a son was born to Frances and Albert in September, 1933, named Kaye Lawrence Dunham.

In 1933 Katherine was chosen to hire and train 150 young blacks for a dance program to be presented at the upcoming Chicago Century of Progress Exposition. As a result of her growing reputation she was invited to a Rosenwald reception.

The Julius Rosenwald Foundation was noted for giving needy artists the money and freedom needed to develop their artistic talents. They had already helped many blacks and represented the kind of support that Katherine had long been seeking. At their reception, attended also by a group of Africans, Katherine met a prominent psychiatrist named Erich Fromm who had come to the United States to raise money to help Jews get out of Europe ahead of the Nazi steamroller. Between this sophisticated European and the young American black dancer a warm, sympathetic understanding sprang up that was to last a lifetime. She believed it was partly through his urging that Mrs. Alfred Rosenwald Stern later attended a recital being given by Katherine's dance group.

Apparently Mrs. Stern liked what she saw. A few days later Katherine received a note from the Rosenwald Foundation inviting her to appear before their board of judges to express her views on Negro dance. If the board thought her ideas worth developing Katherine would receive financial help to further her work. Katherine spent days worrying about how best to present her case.

What could she say to impress them? The board of judges' expressions seemed the epitome of cool, suspended judgment the morning Katherine appeared at the Rosenwald offices. Politely the chairman inquired what was the study Katherine wanted to pursue that might qualify for a Rosenwald grant.

Katherine had her answer ready. She said, "It's a bit difficult to describe, exactly. Do you mind if I show you?"

The chairman faintly nodded. Katherine slipped out of her tailored suit, quickly undressing to the rehearsal costume she wore beneath. This took everyone by surprise. One of the ladies gasped.

Gracefully Katherine pirouetted before them, did an arabesque and acted a lovesick swan. She straightened up and said, "That is the kind of dancing being taught in Chicago."

Then she threw her body into a wild African tribal war dance. She told the board, "That is the way people dance in other places. I want to go where they dance like that. I want to find out why, how it started, and what influence it had on the people. I want to learn something that will help me teach people about the Negro."

The chairman leaned over and asked, "How about

the West Indies?" before he even put the matter to a vote. Katherine won her grant.

But before receiving this good news she had a shocking report about her brother. No one had been unduly worried earlier when Albert had his tonsils out and then suffered sleepless nights. Frances had written that the family physician was being consulted and meanwhile Albert was able to carry on his university classes as usual. But now Albert had suffered a mental breakdown. His wife and many good friends were active on his behalf. The best psychiatrists would see him to recommend treatment. In time there seemed a good chance he might recover.

On this note of hope Katherine Dunham took off for the West Indies. She was twenty-five years old when she won the Rosenwald Foundation travel grant starting her on a career that was to take her several times to Europe, Mexico, and South America, and around the world to Africa, Australia, and Japan. This first year's journey led her to the inspirational wellspring of African dance as it had survived in the Caribbean islands of Jamaica, Martinique, Trinidad—and Haiti.

6

Journey to the Caribbean

*T*he letter from the Julius Rosenwald Foundation awarding a travel fellowship to Katherine Dunham was dated February 15, 1935. They granted her $2,400 of which $500 was to pay tuition and living expenses from March to June, 1935 while she took courses under Dr. Melville Herskovits at Northwestern University. Head of Northwestern's program of African studies, Dr. Herskovits had spent long periods of time in Africa and written many articles and books about its people. The remaining $1,900 of the Rosenwald grant was to pay for Katherine's year in the West Indies, provided Dr. Herskovits found her anthropological studies to be satisfactory and would recommend her for such field work.

Though delighted by this windfall, Katherine at first thought the time she must spend at Northwestern University was a needless delay. She soon learned how well spent this time was to be.

Veteran of many African and Caribbean field trips, Dr. Herskovits believed in the most thorough preparation for such a journey. He taught Katherine to be alert to details of voice tones, food condiments, hand movements, and many other points of observation that add up to a rounded understanding of the people. Herskovits was, Katherine later said, "a fantastic guide for getting to the bottom of things, the heart of the matter."

Studying the people was not all she had to do. She must learn how to report her findings to others when she returned. So Katherine was taught how to operate still and motion picture cameras, how to make records of music and spoken language. For this Dr. Herskovits lent her the old, hand-operated Edison recording machine he had used in Africa. Katherine must learn special scientific terms to describe with accuracy people's physical characteristics. She must know how to care for her equipment so it would not be damaged by rust, dirt, or mold—because once in the field she might not be able to get a machine repaired or to find replacements.

Finally Katherine was given careful instructions in the proper use of many medicines, ointments, and first aid supplies that she must take with her. She learned what health precautions to take to protect herself and how to treat some common diseases of the people she would live among. To help accomplish her work she was given letters of introduction to government officials and scholars in the various islands she would visit. These papers were wrapped in cellophane to protect them against tropical mildew. In all his teachings Dr. Herskovits stressed the importance of patience and caution to the anthropologist.

Her first stop was to be Accompong, a small village in the mountainous northeast part of Jamaica. Dr. Herskovits recommended this community as remaining the most purely African in its ways because it was largely isolated from white man's civilization.

The people of Accompong have a fascinating history. Originally members of the warlike Koromantee tribe on the African west coast, they had been captured in battle by other African tribesmen and sold as slaves to the Spaniards. The Spanish then shipped them to their Caribbean islands to work the sugar cane plantations. When the conquering English later drove the Spaniards out of Jamaica in 1655 the slaves seized this opportunity to run off into the mountains. There they successfully defended themselves against all armies sent after them. Red-coated English soldiers told about forests of trees that suddenly became yelling black warriors who dropped their branches of camouflage to chase the troops back down the mountain.

Called Maroons, probably after the ancient Spanish word meaning mountain top, these people lived for a while by hunting wild boar. As boar became scarce the Maroons developed a farming economy based on African patterns. Eventually the English signed a peace treaty giving them a large grant of land. But the Maroons' reputation for wildness kept the people of the plains from going to see them in the mountains, so they still stayed largely to themselves.

Dr. Herskovits was one of the few who had made even a brief visit, so he was able to give Katherine a letter of introduction to their chief, called the Colonel.

Arriving by boat at the port city of Kingston, Jamaica, Katherine took a train that wound through the upland countryside into the mountains. She could hardly contain her excitement. Kingston looked tiny, miles away on the plain below. As she later described this trip in a book titled *Journey To Accompong*, Katherine felt "as though all the steel-mill drabness of Joliet and the dark winter pinch of Chicago . . . were sliding rapidly downhill and right off Kingston Bay into the ocean." She was glad to let them go.

Maggoty was the small railroad station where she got off to meet the Colonel by pre-arrangement. He was there waiting for her, a slight, leathery man with a formal manner who wore a sun helmet as if it were his badge of office. They drove to the town of White-hall but beyond that there was no road to Accompong. Donkeys carried Katherine and the Colonel the rest of the way, while a string of villagers walked ahead balancing Katherine's extensive luggage on their heads.

The Colonel rode in front of Katherine. She followed with her knees tightly gripping the donkey's sides as they climbed a narrow, rocky upward path through rustling leaves of banana, mango, and breadfruit trees. The warm air brushing her face smelled of tropical flowers and fruits. She was intoxicated by the beauty of the island.

That first night the Colonel had invited Katherine to have dinner and spend the night with him and his family. To her chagrin the Colonel's house turned out to be a two-room hut, which made it necessary for the Colonel and his large family to be crowded into one room so that she might occupy the other. She felt uncomfortable at putting them out this way. She also worried about the fact that she could not easily understand the patois English the Maroons spoke. Their food was too highly seasoned for her; she felt queasy and retired early.

The river rushes that served as her sleeping mat gave off a telltale racket every time she moved and this embarrassed her. She was startled when the sound of Benny Goodman's jazz suddenly blared out into the jungle night.

What had happened, she realized, was that the Maroons got into her records after she went to bed. Katherine wondered if they would soon take her over as casually. She found these amiable brown people difficult to approach. Though they no longer deserved the fierce reputation they'd once been given, the polite and hospitable Maroons now seemed menacing in a different way. Instead of answering her questions they asked a lot of their own about Katherine and her equipment. If that continued, how could she learn about *their* ways? Worst of all the Maroons seemed so cool and self-possessed that Katherine simply couldn't imagine them dancing.

The sleeping mat crackled again as she tossed and turned trying to decide what to do. Feeling homesick, discouraged, and lonely she wondered what Dr. Herskovits would recommend under these circumstances.

He might tell her simply to relax, Katherine thought. Perhaps she should put brakes on her impatient curiosity to witness ceremonials or dances and adopt a slower, more natural approach to understanding the people. Surely the Maroons wouldn't resent her if she lived quietly among them and wrote down each day's events as they happened. Relieved by these thoughts, Katherine finally dozed off to sleep.

The next day she was greatly cheered by news that the Colonel had found her a house of her own, vacant because the Maroon who owned it was temporarily away. It had two rooms—a living room and a bedroom. A separate hut served as kitchen, with a cooking fireplace on the ground. For food preparation and for washing dishes there was an outdoor table. These were the usual Maroon domestic arrangements.

Rent was $1.25 a month. For another $1.25 Katherine hired a woman who would live with her and help her with the housekeeping, shopping, and cooking. Mai came from another tribe. All Maroon women were customarily too occupied with their own houses, children, and fields to work for someone else.

Already Katherine had grasped something of the Maroon way of life from these simple business transactions. She learned more on a morning walk with the Colonel as he greeted family and friends around the village and explained their customs of kinship.

Courtship leading to pregnancy before marriage was common among Accompong people, she learned. Usually the man and the pregnant woman married. But if he was already married or if she didn't want him for a husband, the Maroon man still regarded the baby as his responsibility and gave it the same affection and support as his own legitimate children. This ceased only if the baby's mother married someone else, when it was expected her new husband would adopt her babies as the equal of those they might have together.

Every baby received a gift of a coconut or breadfruit tree. Under this tree the baby's navel cord and afterbirth were planted, and that tree with its fruit belonged to the child for the rest of his life.

The Colonel was being so cordial and informative that morning Katherine couldn't resist lightly reminding him that she was greatly interested in Maroon dances. In particular she wanted to see the old Koromantee War Dance they'd brought with them from Africa.

Without promising anything the Colonel nodded

and politely asked Katherine if she would like to have a refreshing drink. Suddenly she heard him shouting at the boy he had dispatched with a machete to cut down a coconut for its milk. "Here you! What you think! That no me tree, you know that me brother's tree!"

Shamefaced, the boy clambered down and moved to a tree belonging to the Colonel. Property rights were strongly enforced by fatherly discipline, as Katherine was to observe many times, but children were rarely struck. The most effective punishment seemed to be public ridicule. A withering remark was: "For shame, sir, you too rude!" As the adults scoffed at lazy workers in their farming group, so the youngsters ridiculed one another's bad behavior.

That night, and on many nights thereafter, Katherine stayed up late writing notes based on her observations of Maroon life. Her kerosene lamp, burning long as she worked, was considered a luxury by the villagers whose hours followed the rising and setting of the sun. As she blew the lamp out, Katherine reminded herself she must wait quietly for events to naturally unfold. In the morning, waking later than the others, she enjoyed picking sweet-smelling gardenias from the bushes in her own yard to put on her breakfast table.

So the time passed pleasantly enough until, on the fifth day, Katherine heard there was to be a dance that evening. Her patience was being rewarded. All day the village buzzed in pleasurable anticipation.

When the dark night fell, candles and bobbing lanterns lighted the villagers' way uphill to the Parade, a flat grassy field on top of a rise. Katherine, following with Mai, noticed that the women were dressed in long gingham shifts, belted at the waist, with snowy white kerchiefs bound around their heads. Men wore khaki trousers or blue denims and some had straw hats. Almost all were barefoot.

The fiddler hired for the occasion came from Whitehall. He repeatedly banged his tin cup for more rum while complaining angrily about his fee. This worried Katherine until she was assured that this was his customary behavior.

After warming his bow a while, the fiddler launched into a lively number, tapping his feet. Men lined up, bowing low to women opposite, who curtseyed. Soon Katherine recognized the dance as a Maroon version of the early English quadrille!

This was not the kind of dance she had expected. Where were the exotic customs the Maroons must have carried from their jungle past? She was further surprised to notice that a gray-haired woman in her sixties, named Miss Mary, was a favorite dancing partner. She was not the only older woman apparently preferred by the men. When Katherine remarked on this she was told the older women's longer years of practice frequently improved their dancing artistry. They did, indeed, move with a lithe grace and strength astonishing for their years.

Katherine longed to join in the dancing but it

wasn't until the sixth movement that the Colonel asked her to be his partner. She gave herself over to the music in a hip-swinging number called the Shay-Shay that she suspected was entirely a Maroon invention.

By now everyone was having a wonderful time. The dancers occasionally paused for a drink of rum or to "catch a breath," and the younger children watched, wide-eyed, until they fell asleep.

The following morning the Colonel's grandchild, Priscilla, came bearing a gift basket of fresh pineapples and bananas for Katherine. Close on her heels followed a villager named Old Marie. It seemed everyone was talking about the way Katherine had taken part in the dancing and since Old Marie hadn't been there she wanted to hear all about it. Obligingly Katherine acted out the story. She rose and bowed with a flourish as the men had done. Then she took the part of the ladies curtseying back before launching into a lively demonstration of the steps they did together.

Old Marie and Priscilla could hardly catch their breaths for laughing. Then Old Marie demonstrated a few steps, seizing young Priscilla as her partner. This started a kind of party that lasted most of the morning. When word spread about what a good time they'd had, other villagers called on Katherine. They danced, listened to her jazz records, gossiped, and told stories. The ice was broken. Katherine found herself accepted as part of village life.

Among all her new friends Katherine had several favorites. Ba (for Brother) Teddy was a husky, soft-spoken member of the Colonel's governing council who answered many questions about Accompong ways. Sixty-year-old Ba Weeyums was a bent, gnarled, natural-born comic whose capering imitation of a monkey playing a violin sent his audiences into knee-slapping paroxysms of laughter. He also told animal fables.

Katherine recorded one of them, about a race between a turtle and a horse to get to Kingston. No matter how hard the horse galloped he seemed always to find the turtle ahead of him at each mile post. Actually what the horse saw was a series of turtles cunningly placed along the way the day before the race. The horse finally dropped dead of exhaustion.

This reminded Katherine, she said, of a story from home about a race between a hare and a tortoise. Ba Weeyums wanted to hear that story. After Katherine told it he shook his head in violent disagreement. The two stories weren't at all alike, he said, pointing out that "The turtle don't win because this horse go to sleep. No, sir. The turtle win 'cause eem *outsmart* the horse! That's different!"

Another special friend was Hannah, an independent woman who showed that even in this patriarchal society a single woman had her rights. When her common-law husband left for the lowlands Hannah had chosen to remain alone, managing her fields with the help of her children and other relatives. Even if

Hannah should later marry, Katherine learned, her fields would not automatically become her husband's property, but would still belong to her, to be inherited by her older daughters.

As Katherine came to know her new friends better she inquired about religious rites they may have seen their fathers or grandfathers practice. The Maroons looked back at her blankly. Katherine could not make up her mind whether their ignorance was real or pretended, part of a plot to keep any and all outsiders from knowing their secrets. Perhaps Ba Weeyums was trying in his own fashion to give her a clue when she was led to the discovery at the graveyard.

It happened this way. One evening a group of people were gathered at Katherine's house listening to her jazz records when a different kind of music was heard nearby. A chorus of men was singing a refrain that Katherine had never heard before. Remembering that sickly Miss Cross had died that day, Katherine thought this might be a song of mourning for her, and she wanted to hear it better. Excusing herself, Katherine went with Hannah down to the graveyard where the singing seemed to come from.

In the misty night the two women saw half a dozen grave diggers singing while they scooped a hole in the wet clay with their machetes. Drunkenly reeling and falling over themselves the men were covered with yellow mud. Towering over them on the edge of the hole stood Ba Weeyums. He looked like a wicked little goblin, holding a cane in one raised hand and a communal bottle of rum in the other.

Katherine's nerves tingled as she looked into the grave. Slanting off from the usual rectangle was a tunnel hacked out of the earth. She recognized this as the traditional grave of the Koromantee and Diola Africans who dig the tunnel to confuse the dead person and prevent him from finding his way back among the living. So there *were* still ties to their African past after all!

However, the Maroons' explanation for the way the grave was dug was, "They hit a rock." Katherine wondered if the villagers had completely forgotten the origins of their own customs. At least they were able to tell her the song they had been singing was Koromantee, as Katherine had guessed. But why did the Colonel never set a date for the Koromantee War Dance? If she could not break through this barrier Katherine felt she would be a failure as an anthropologist.

She appealed to her special friends again for help. Warming to her interest, they told her about the ancient musical instruments they had once used and promised to get her some of them. She collected a bamboo flute, a gourd rattle, and later a horn. Ba Weeyums made her a tambourine. Another villager promised to make a goombay, a square wooden drum that once accompanied all Maroon dances. Katherine's heart sank when she heard these old-time dances had not been done for so long that the last drum had decayed into dust.

Though she continued to make inquiries, in the days that followed she was unable to find out anything else about the old traditions. Soon she must leave Jamaica to make further studies at other Caribbean islands. Katherine was melancholy when the time came to pack. She had formed many genuine ties of affection with the people. Into her luggage went such Accompong mementos as a river reed basket, a cedarwood bowl, a woven hammock, and her musical instruments. Almost finished with packing, she realized she still didn't have the goombay she had been promised. She decided to find out what was delaying it.

As soon as she stepped outdoors she heard the drum. At first she couldn't tell where the sound came from. Then she noticed a few kerosene torches flickering in the underbrush at the bottom of the hill. Her heart beat faster. She crept closer and came upon a ring of villagers paying rapt attention to a dance being performed in the center. There was something menacing in the way Miss Mary and an old man circled one another seductively to the beat of a square wooden drum that Katherine knew at once must be her goombay. The expert player of the drum was none other than Ba Weeyums and standing tall next to him was Ba Teddy.

Katherine felt so betrayed by these two old friends that her eyes filled with tears. They knew well of her interest in their ancient rituals, and this strange dance was surely one of them. Yet they had not invited her to come—and furthermore they were using her drum!

The drum stopped as her two friends approached. In soft, apologetic tones they explained that they were on their way to deliver the drum when, unplanned, they decided to play it once more and old Miss Mary had started to dance. Ordinarily the Colonel sharply discouraged such dances but tonight they didn't have to worry because the Colonel was away on a trip.

People began to drift off, and putting her hurt feelings aside, Katherine asked quickly what could be done to make it all start up again. Ba Weeyums told her that the goombay needed to be baptized with rum. He said shrewdly, "Don't no goombay talk like him should talk if him no had rum."

Katherine immediately sent for her rum supply, urging the people to stay. She was warned that she must not talk about anything she was about to witness. They must try not to wake up the rest of the village and not stay too long.

The rum came and Ba Weeyums, tilting the bottle, took a swallow and spat on the drum. Then he poured a few drops on the ground for the god. The goombay responded in wonderful full-throated tones as Ba Weeyums stroked or struck the taut goatskin with his calloused hands. The dance resumed. Miss Mary, with a set facial expression but a body wonderfully liquid, circled tauntingly around the old man who squatted with his arms held out as if trying to embrace her.

Ba Teddy whispered explanations to Katherine.

The old man was the "doctor" and Miss Mary was the "duppy" or dead woman the doctor wanted to get in his power to command her lifetime knowledge of black magic. Though he wooed her the doctor was afraid, as evidenced by the trembling fingers of his open hands. At first the aggressor in this evil courtship, the doctor became the pursued. Terrified at what he'd started by calling this woman from the dead, the doctor then tried to retreat.

The dance became a tense life-and-death struggle for ascendancy. The onlookers breathed more rapidly, watching it. When Miss Mary seemed to triumph and leaned threateningly over the quivering doctor Katherine wanted to look away. At that point, with one sharp blow on the drum, the dance ended.

Everyone drew a deep breath of relief. Wiping the sweat from his face, Ba Teddy told Katherine it was best if she asked no more questions. He said, "That dance mixed up with bad business. Better for misses if she forget."

Ba' Weeyums beat the drum to a different rhythm and two men hopped around each other, bobbing their heads in imitation of a cockfight. Laughter relaxed everybody. At last, in answer to Katherine's urging, the old people agreed to perform the Koromantee war dance.

There was nothing so terrible about it despite the Colonel's caution. Crouching, feinting, and leaping the dancers started by attacking an imaginary enemy in the jungle. The women shook rattles and the men brandished sticks. Sometimes the women shook the shoulders of the men to work them up to greater bravery. At the end, dancing with arms around their partner's waists, in a strong resemblance to the Highland Fling, the women waved kerchiefs snatched from their heads as if in celebration of expected victory. Katherine could not understand why the Colonel had forbade it. Could he possibly have been afraid it might reawaken old feelings of warlike hostility?

Exhausted by this strenuous workout, so different from the "set" dances of the Parade, the people finally went home. Carrying her goombay, Katherine happily climbed the hill with Ba Teddy and Ba Weeyums. She knew that along the way people were talking behind closed shutters about the evening escapade and how they mustn't anger the Colonel by letting him find out.

But it wasn't only the Colonel, Katherine had observed, who wanted to forget the old ways. She noticed that most of the young people had not joined in the dancing. They seemed disapproving that Katherine took part. Here, as elsewhere, the youth weren't interested in continuing a people's tradition; they wanted to be as "progressive" as the rest of the world.

In this simple agricultural economy—where a man held land only so long as he worked it and no acreage could be bought or sold—there was no poverty and almost no crime. Yet many of the young people left the peaceable security and friendliness of the village for the uncertainties of Kingston because they wanted to be part of the modern world.

The mountain community of Accompong was not so isolated as it seemed. To find what she wanted Katherine would have to look somewhere else. Three days later, after many tearful farewells, Katherine boarded a ship bound for other West Indian islands.

7

African Gods in Haiti

*K*atherine's journey took her
next to Martinique where she saw the fighting dance
called Ag'Ya and heard stories about Zombie activities
on the island. Mainly, however, she concentrated on
the islanders' social dances rather than their religion
or folklore, as a change from Accompong.

Moving on to Trinidad she began to investigate
Shango. An official in the Trinidad Education Department had told Katherine that participants in a
Shango ceremony went into a "trance-like state in-
duced partly by auto-suggestion and partly by rum."
He said that in this trance they danced imitations of
various animals, most spectacularly the snake. And
he recommended it as "one of the few survivors of

the original African dance." The dances were held openly, every Saturday night, but the religious ceremonies connected with Shango were "held in strictest secrecy."

With a friend's help, Katherine met a Shango priest who agreed to let her take part in the ceremony. From the window of a hut, where she was supposedly undergoing purification, Katherine watched the rites begin. A white rooster, held upside down and desperately struggling for its life, was about to have its throat slit by a knife-wielding priest as a sacrifice to the Shango gods. Katherine started to take motion pictures of the event, but the alert priest heard the whirring of the camera.

Throwing rooster and knife into the air, the priest angrily charged Katherine's hut and wrenched the camera out of her hands. Only her friend's intercession saved her, she felt, from possible worse treatment. She was trembling with fright. The experience discouraged her from using the motion picture camera during the rest of her Caribbean journey.

It did not, however, discourage her search for ancient African religious rites. Much of the zest she had for this search was due to her anthropological outlook and training as well as her interest in dance. But there were other motivations that went deeper.

Africans who were torn from their own land and taken as slaves to other countries suffered a sense of deprivation that has been inherited by many of their descendants. Katherine was one of those who felt shorn of her true identity, who yearned to know "what we are really like [as against] what we have been made into by slavery and/or colonialism." She wanted to learn "how to care for our lares and penates, our own household gods."

Dr. Herskovits feared that such a search to discover primitive jungle gods and rites might be dangerous for his young anthropology student. He sent a warning letter to Katherine on November 11, 1935 at Hotel de Paris, Port of Spain, Trinidad. "There is only one thing that bothers me and that is the danger that you will try to do more than your strength permits."

But Katherine was determined to continue her investigations in her own way. She moved on to Haiti for her longest stay and most serious involvement in local religious ceremonies.

Haiti had won its independence from France in 1804 after a bloody revolution and the massacre of the whites. Under black emperors and dictators the country was then reft by a series of civil wars that led to anarchy and bankruptcy in the twentieth century. To keep European countries from entering Haiti to collect their debts or claim possession, the United States stepped in. They first took over the corrupt Haiti customs receivership in 1905. Then the United States Marines landed during World War I to effect a compulsory protectorate, but their behavior left much to be desired, and they were never welcome. True, American know-how had improved financial conditions, but violation of the country's sovereignty was bound to be strongly resented. Finally world opinion, supported by a Senate investigating committee, led to the United States withdrawal in 1934.

When Katherine arrived in early 1936 tourism was being encouraged under President Sténio Vincent, and the form of government was modeled on democracy. French was still the language spoken and the culture preferred by the sophisticated mulatto ruling classes in the capital city of Port-au-Prince. In the back country dwelled the more purely black peasants who made up 90 percent of the population. Poor and illiterate, their lives had barely been touched by any of the changes or improvements introduced by white European civilization. There was no Colonel to tell them not to practice the old religious rites. That they did so was recorded in William Seabrook's book *Magic Island*. But he was white and saw it from the outside looking in, as had Melville Herskovits, Katherine's teacher, in another study of Haiti. Katherine meant to go deeper, to become a part of that religion as an insider among her own people.

She established her headquarters at the Hotel Excelsior in Port-au-Prince, renting a tiny one-room cupola on the roof. From her balcony she looked over a small park bright with flowering poinsettia and frangipani bushes. She also had a view of a lower balcony on which, one morning soon after her arrival, she saw two men standing. They began talking to one another from balcony to balcony.

The portly man, wearing a bathrobe and thick sunglasses, she knew to be Senator Zépherin, another resident of the hotel whom she had previously met. The younger, well-dressed stranger beside him was introduced as Dumarsais Estimé, head of the Haitian Chamber of Deputies. His serious demeanor and broad forehead poignantly reminded Katherine of her brother. Following that first meeting Estimé called on her many times, put his car and chauffeur at her disposal for sightseeing, and eventually became a close, cherished friend.

But that morning when Katherine met Estimé she did not want to begin her visit to Haiti by cultivating the further acquaintance of any government officials. Instead she preferred to start off by using a note of introduction from Dr. Herskovits addressed to a white American former Marine and ship's pharmacist named "Doc" Reeser. Remaining in Haiti after the United States withdrawal, Reeser had become head of the island's insane asylum and ministered to its sick. He lived with a dark Haitian peasant woman named Cécile in the back section of the country, the area that most interested Katherine.

While most country people lived very primitively, Doc had introduced a few amenities. He put beds in Cécile's hut to replace the mats spread over the ground on which country people habitually slept. He brought in sheets and kerosene lamps. Otherwise Cécile's house was similar to the others in the small community of huts, called a compound, where she lived.

Katherine became a frequent visitor there and began to meet the country people. Again, she soon had her favorites among these new friends. One was a stout, earthy, motherly woman named Téoline. By contrast another friend, Dégrasse, was almost elegant in manner, with quiet ways and a slender body. Both were priestesses in Vaudun, popularly called Voodoo.

Though intensely interested in these beliefs and practices, Katherine knew it wouldn't be proper to question them or ask to become one of them. All she could do was indicate her sincere interest and then wait patiently and hope for acceptance.

With others at Cécile's compound Katherine ate from the common cookpot, compared and exchanged cosmetics, and danced far into the night, learning the Haitian way to do the Congo, Meringue, Rumba, and Bolero. Sharing so many activities helped to deepen Katherine's new friendships.

Many mornings, typing her field notes in her hotel room, Katherine would somehow get the message that Téoline, Dégrasse, or Cécile were waiting in the park below. It might be a feeling she had, or sometimes a whispered word from the hotel maid as she brought in a cup of burnt, bitter coffee. Going out on her balcony Katherine would see Dégrasse standing by the donkey that had brought her in, or Téoline sitting on a park bench, or Cécile waving from the street. Each of them knew that the owners of the hotel, the respectable Rouzier sisters, would be furious if they tried to enter.

The Haitian social system was based on color, with

lighter skins the most preferred, as Katherine Dunham explains in her book about Haiti titled *Island Possessed*. Very dark people like Téoline, Cécile, and Dégrasse were on the bottom of the social ladder. By even knowing these people from the back country Katherine put her own social reputation in jeopardy. She was protected to some degree, however, by Dr. Herskovits' letter of introduction to the Rouzier sisters that established her as a scholar and a lady. Also, her skin color proclaimed her to be mulatto or "griffon"—certainly with some mixture of white blood—which was favorable in Haitian eyes.

Paradoxically a purely white man such as the handsome blonde Englishman, Fred Allsop, was unacceptable because he was considered totally non-Haitian. That he held a job and therefore ranked as laborer in the Haitian hierarchy was also counted against him. Fred was chief mechanic and assistant manager at the only garage in town and was a friend of Doc Reeser, through whom Katherine met him. She valued his witty, intelligent, congenial companionship but she knew the Rouzier sisters did not approve of him either. Such considerations never deterred Katherine from seeing whom she pleased.

Whenever her friends from the Cul-de-Sac back country turned up, Katherine would unhesitatingly fly down the hotel stairs to greet them, openly showing her affection. They always brought her the latest news from the bush, whether it was about a special Saturday night dance to be held, someone's sickness, a budding romance, or some minor religious celebration she might like to attend. For by now they were beginning to satisfy her curiosity about these things.

So far Katherine had witnessed only small, unimportant ceremonies. One day she received word about a more significant event. A leading bush priest had died and a Congo ceremony would be held for his return from the dead to name his successor.

Her trips to such religious ceremonies had to be kept secret from the upper class Haitians Katherine knew, so when Katherine again borrowed Dumarsais Estimé's car and chauffeur to travel the fifty miles to the dead priest's compound, she claimed it was for a sightseeing trip.

The roads were bad, with few signposts along the way. At sunset they seemed to be lost. The chauffeur stopped the car and asked Katherine what they should do next. As soon as the motor was shut off the sound of drumming and singing could be heard somewhere nearby. Katherine opened her car door to hear better and this automatically turned on the overhead light. In its illumination she saw the chauffeur huddled small behind the wheel, looking badly frightened at whatever story he heard the drums telling.

Infected by his fear, Katherine was about to order him to drive back towards town when she noticed a man with a light moving towards them. Mahogany brown in skin color, the man's chest was bare and he wore red kerchiefs tied around his neck and each arm. Smiling, he spoke in French, addressing Katherine by name and offering her the hospitality of his house until the time came to take her to the ceremony she wished to see. His name was Antoine.

The chauffeur hastened to get away but Katherine followed Antoine over the brow of a hill to his hut. As she stepped through the doorway Katherine froze, smelling the acrid odor of snake. It was a python about eight feet long, eyes glistening and tongue darting as he stirred on the crossbeam above her head.

There are no poisonous snakes in Haiti. Katherine knew that, and also that pythons are kept by many country people as pets because they eat rodents and thus help protect the family food supply. Still, she couldn't help shuddering at the snake's presence even as she saw it settle back quietly on its perch.

Sinking almost in a faint to a seat on the floor matting she gratefully accepted the offer of a cup of sweet, thick coffee. While waiting for word that the ceremony would begin, Antoine said he would tell her fortune with cards. He narrated incidents about her past life and delivered messages from her long-dead mother. As to the future, he said the cards warned Katherine against personal and professional jealousies that would threaten her peace.

She had already experienced some of that. A few fellow students envied her travel grant; Fred Allsop resented Dumarsais Estimé, and vice versa. As long as she remained married to Jordis McCoo, Katherine supposed that gave him the right to be jealous of every other man.

But what was really on her mind was something she'd told no one else in Haiti—her brother's mental breakdown. She couldn't help feeling that the stresses young Albert suffered long ago working in the darkness under the massive threat of the dust wheel, and his tense relationship with his father, had played a part in causing the torments he now endured at Washington's St. Elizabeth Hospital. Here, in this remote hut on a dark plain, she was moved to talk about the pity and the waste of it. Grieving for the "abrupt interruption to his intellectual brilliance" she wished passionately that she could do something to make him well again. Antoine tried to comfort her as she started to cry, saying that perhaps the African gods could be persuaded to intervene in her brother's favor.

They were interrupted by a messenger who came to the door of the hut. After talking to him, Antoine explained that the old priest had returned to the land of the living with great reluctance, for he was very tired. Katherine, a stranger, must stay outside the dead man's hut in order not to upset his spirit.

They walked down the hill to where space had been reserved for Katherine at the window of the hut. Through the smudged glass pane she saw a crowded room, smoky with burning incense. On the bed a very old man, his jaw bound shut by a kerchief wrapped around his head, was sitting up with his arm stiffly pointing to a young man who knelt before him. This was his nephew, chosen to be his earthly successor.

The nephew climbed on the bed to place his forehead against the dead man's brow. In the eerie silence —all previous drumming and moaning having stopped —there was a sound like a sigh as the dead man fell back. His successor kissed the dead priest's withered hand and the people broke out in cries of celebration and rejoicing.

There would be more to see tomorrow, Antoine said as they walked back to his hut. This had been only the first day of the ceremony. Given a sleeping mat in the same place she'd sat before, Katherine saw the snake still curled up overhead. She drenched a handkerchief with cologne and held it to her nose to drown out the snake's odor.

But she couldn't get to sleep. During the night her restlessness roused the snake who started to uncoil, presumably to slither down to the ground. Whether owing to her fear of the snake, the evening's emotional experiences, or something in the coffee she'd drunk, Katherine had to rush outside because she felt violently sick.

To excuse herself from staying for the rest of the night, Katherine invented an early morning appointment back in Port-au-Prince. Antoine did not hold this sudden change of plans against her. Indeed, he probably regarded her emotional and physical distress as proof that the African gods were getting through to her, in which case fear is an understandable and usual reaction. He gave Katherine a guide with whom she hiked through a heavy thunderstorm to an army outpost. There she made a distress telephone call—

not to Estimé who had loaned her his car, but to Fred Allsop.

His reaction was so explosive Katherine had to hold the phone away from her ear. Fred loudly cursed the needless risks to her health and safety Katherine took on these expeditions. He was still bawling her out as they drove back to the city in his rattling old Chevrolet. Katherine meekly accepted his scolding and wearily climbed up to her penthouse to take a potassium permanganate bath before the hotel maid came with her morning coffee.

She dreaded the interview that awaited her when she next saw Dumarsais Estimé because she knew he, like Fred, would disapprove of her evening's outing. For a week she did not hear a word from him. When Estimé finally came there was no doubting his angry displeasure, but his attitude differed from Fred Allsop's.

Estimé took Katherine to the city's slums. She had been there before with Fred, to talk to boatmen at nearby docks, and they had listened to the sailors' tales of what life was like in the strange coastal towns they came from. But Estimé's trip along the waterfront had another purpose. He asked Katherine to look at how the people had to fetch water from public fountains in whatever discarded containers they could scrounge, and how they were forced to use narrow alleys outside their cardboard huts for garbage disposal and toilet. He spoke about how they suffered constantly from such diseases as yaws, elephantiasis, and intestinal parasites of all kinds. Unable to feed their children these people sold their sons and daughters to be servants in Haitian hotels or private homes. At least in such places they knew the children would have a roof overhead, be given leftover food to eat, and castoff clothes to wear.

"These are the realities of Haitian life," he told Katherine soberly. Her interest in Congo and Voodoo ceremonies infuriated him because he believed such religious frenzies misdirected the energies the people should be using to work for political and social change. On this point he would agree with Marx's statement, "Religion is the opiate of the people."

Estimé's dreams were to give all children an elementary school education and to teach them skills with which they could earn wages. He wanted the government to clean up the market places that spread diseases, give everyone shoes to keep their feet from picking up parasitical worms, and build decent housing.

Katherine loved Estimé for his humanistic idealism, which she shared. But she said that just as Estimé must concentrate on his job as statesman, so must she pursue her career in anthropology and the dance. It was not proper or possible for her, as an American citizen, to take part in Haitian political life. She was not in Haiti to change things but to learn things. The old religion was part of her study. They parted amicably, each walking a different path.

During the weeks that followed her experiences at

Antoine's compound, Katherine found herself the focus of special attentions. Seats would be reserved for her at religious ceremonies and someone placed nearby to explain the rituals. Again her patience, learned in Accompong, was rewarded. She was invited to be among the next group of people to undergo the ceremony of initiation into Voodoo.

To prepare for this event Katherine had to collect offerings for the gods—white baptismal clothes and veil, blue and white trade beads, Florida and barley water, strawberry soda, sugar cookies, and eggs. Other offerings she must make were numerous herbs, roots, and powders—and two live cocks.

The ceremonies began with the initiates spending three days and nights on the floor of a hut where they were to undergo purification and await visitations from the gods. There were nine initiates, male and female, ranging in age from seven to seventy, lying closely together fitted into one another like spoons. The clap of a hand or a bell ringing told them when they might turn over together to the other side or get up to attend to basic necessities.

This was a reliving of the experiences their ancestors had suffered packed into the lower decks of slave ships that brought them from Africa, when such signals had told them when they might turn, stretch, or march on deck for exercise. Katherine's stomach growled with hunger from the imposed fasting, but she found she could swallow only token portions of the sacred foods that were brought them. She was sweating profusely in the heat, as were the others. In their hair all of them wore a paste of eggs and corn-meal mixed with feathers, herbs, and sacrificial blood and bound with a bandana. In their ears was the continual quiet beating of drums meant to wash out all irrelevant thoughts or memories from their heads.

Her bones aching with pain, Katherine felt her dis-comfort overcame even her apprehensions. Much of the time she yearned to be somewhere else—on a fishing boat sailing over the sparkling sea, or driving with Fred Allsop in the bright moonlight along the winding coastal road, or even back home in Joliet which she later said "indicated a state of total eclipse."

Katherine wondered miserably where was the promised ecstasy? Her supreme moment was yet to come, but meanwhile—whether despite or because of the extraordinary discomfort—there were moments of reverence, of suspense, of reaching feelings that had not been touched before.

The first visitation happened during the night to a woman who was sleeping next to Katherine. The woman jerked convulsively and Katherine woke to see Téoline tap the woman's shoulder. Speaking as a priestess, Téoline announced, "Papa Guedé has come. Rise and greet him and become one of us."

A Voodoo priest, representing Papa Guedé, came in wearing the Haitian god's costume of a top hat and black frock coat, carrying a cane, and smoking a pipe. This god, whose eyes are habitually bloodshot and who always smells of rum and tobacco, is known for his outrageously lewd behavior. He speaks rudely in a nasal voice.

Whenever anyone in life behaves so vulgarly, the Voodoo culture speaks of such a person as being "possessed" by Papa Guedé, with whom everyone sooner or later seems to get acquainted. Feared as one of the gods of death and cemeteries, Papa Guedé often has to be drummed away in a hip-grinding dance of appeasement. Worn out from her first brush with him, the woman in front of Katherine returned to fall into a heavy sleep.

The second day's visitation fell upon a ten-year-old girl who joyfully rose at the entrance of the goddess Erzulie, represented by Téoline now dressed in a white satin slip covered with spangles. A crown of paste diamonds on her head and a fixed smile on her lips similar to the expression on many plaster statues of the Virgin Mary, Téoline led the child in a slow dance. Katherine tried, but she couldn't think how to choreograph the grace of their movements.

Her mind was still on this when her own particular god entered the hut. This was the serpent god, Damballa, perhaps chosen because of her strong reaction to snakes. Damballa appeared in the person of a drummer who slid across the floor on his belly, hands clasped behind his back and tongue darting. The usual offering for snakes is a saucer holding a mound of flour on which a raw egg is perched. The drummer slid to the saucer, broke the egg with his chin, and sucked the egg.

Katherine thought the white flour sticking around the boy's mouth made him look like a minstrel show comic. Nervously she wanted to laugh. But she knew this visit was meant to signify honor and approval of her as an initiate. She didn't have to do anything in return if the spirit didn't move her. Hypocrisy was strongly disapproved of by the priests and they would notice if she was pretending. So Katherine kept her place, soberly watching the drummer until he backed out of the hut.

As the complicated ceremony went on the initiates learned about holy keepsakes and gestures. They were taught prayers to appease unknown powers, to win their help in achieving success, love, good health, and fortune.

On the third day the initiates were allowed to move around and change into their new white clothes to be "wedded" to their particular gods. Katherine was glad to be able to bend and stretch and brush her teeth.

Finally they all went blinking into the sunlight for the celebration. A feast was in preparation and a crowd of onlookers awaited them including Doc Reeser, Cécile, and Fred Allsop. As the drums sounded and the dancing began there was one dance that strongly affected Katherine. Done with shoulders spasmodically hunching forward and then jerked back rhythmically the dance gave Katherine an overwhelming feeling of ecstasy.

This was when she felt the gods truly entered her.

The Haitians describe it as being "possessed." It struck her that this was the true purpose of dance— these exhilarations and releases of tension shared by a community, bringing people closer together. By contrast the white man's ballroom dancing seemed to be a form of status-seeking in a competitive society.

Her jubilation came to an abrupt end. She was shocked to see a boy, seemingly possessed by the serpent god Damballa, bite into the neck of a live chicken and drink its blood. In her childhood Katherine had been a tender doctor to wounded cats, dogs, and birds. She was never able to accept the Haitian callousness towards animals and their ritual requirements of animal sacrifice. Feeling quite sick, she fled the ceremonies to find refuge in Cécile's hut. Throwing up what little food was in her stomach, she fell asleep.

Hours later she was awakened by Fred Allsop who brought her, as she later told it, "a ham sandwich on a long piece of French bread, buttered, and I secretly blessed him for this reminder of a world outside the Vaudun."

Shaken and exhausted, Katherine returned to the back country only once, a week later, for the ritual removal of the tangled mass of cornmeal, eggs, feathers, and herbs still in her hair. Otherwise she stayed close to her hotel room writing up her notes and preparing for a dance concert she had promised to put on at the Rex Theatre in Port-au-Prince.

Katherine dreaded the prospect of giving a solo performance but the manager demanded it for the entire second half of the evening's entertainment. "No country performers, no Voodoo dances," he insisted firmly when Katherine suggested sharing the stage with dancers from Cécile's compound. "None of that kind of thing, not at the Rex."

The first half of the program featured an aging blonde French singer, formerly a star of the Opera de Paris in France. Then came Katherine's turn. To avoid monotony she planned to show a variety of dance styles with many changes of costume. For her first number she wore a white tulle dress and did a classical ballet. Then she performed a gypsy dance from the operetta *Countess Maritza*. Next Katherine dance-mimed the part of a nurse vainly trying to put a baby to sleep. The grand climax was a Spanish dance in full costume including tortoise shell comb in her hair, purple high heel shoes, and the castanets Argentina had given her.

It was a sophisticated program that satisfied some deep esthetic hunger of the Haitian elite. There were bravas and loud applause and Katherine was deluged with flowers, phone calls, and invitations. All her strange excursions into the bush were magnanimously excused by her audience as "artistic temperament."

Having already made friends with the peasantry, Katherine now found herself in the very good graces of the Haitian aristocracy. Her total acceptance by all classes of Haitians seemed especially wonderful to her in view of the rebuffs she had sometimes suffered in the United States.

Only a week was left before Katherine must leave

Haiti in time to arrive at the University of Chicago before summer examinations began. She revisited the back country to say her farewells. It was then she learned that though she had reserved a row of seats for her country friends at her dance concert, only Cécile had attended. Mistaking the intermission for the end of the show, Cécile left after seeing only the first half of the program. Waking everyone in her compound when she returned, she excitedly told them about the "service" she had witnessed in which Mademoiselle Katherine was completely "possessed" by La Sirene, the blonde sea goddess who sings demands for sailor's offerings in return for granting them safe sea passage.

None of the people in the compound would listen to Katherine's explanation of the blonde French woman opera singer who appeared on the first half of the show. They remained full of pride and awe that Katherine had such a remarkable spiritual visitation.

One day, after another visit to a Voodoo priest in the hills above the city, Katherine walked back to Port-au-Prince. On the way she joined a group of women cooling their feet in a brook. These women worked as portresses, carrying produce from the hills to the city. They chatted and laughed together. Before going on, Katherine drank from a sweet spring originating in a property called Habitation Leclerc. Once Napoleon's sister, Pauline Bonaparte Leclerc, had lived there. Then a French General named Rochambeau committed terrible atrocities against Haitian soldiers and slaves on the grounds. Since then, the mansion had been left to crumble. People said the place was haunted and no one wanted to buy the property.

That may have been the moment when Katherine realized that she'd like to have a home on this enchantingly beautiful island someday. Nibbling wild carrots and watercress as she resumed her walk down the hill, Katherine toyed with the idea that the haunted Habitation Leclerc might be bought for a reasonable price if she could ever get some money together.

The period of time spent in Haiti had been, she felt, most important to her personal and professional development. As at Accompong, Katherine made friends there she found hard to leave. One of her last glimpses of Haiti, as her Royal Netherlands boat steamed out of the harbor, was of the ornate pink cathedral and the Leclerc property. She was filled with that kind of sadness that comes, she said, "of always leaving a part of myself behind, still knowing that moving on is inevitable."

8

A Change of Direction

*O*n the ship taking her home, Katherine walked the decks and pondered her future. She knew she would be expected by Dr. Herskovits to pursue an academic career, continuing her field work and lecturing to students, perhaps even becoming a distingiushed anthropologist like himself.

But Katherine wanted to continue with her dancing, and especially to bring black dance the attention it deserved. The place to do that was on the stage, not in the classroom. From past experience, however, she knew the uncertainties of trying to make her living by this means. Teaching would offer her far greater financial security. She wished she could talk this all over with her brother, but he was still wrestling with his own devils in St. Elizabeth's Hospital. For the moment, she felt obliged to follow in the expected academic routine, and to present tangible results of her grant.

Going before the Julius Rosenwald Foundation, who had funded her trip, Katherine talked about her experiences. She showed them pictures, played recordings, and danced the shoulder dance to the Voodoo god, Damballa. The drummer-accompanist for her dancing was her proud professor, Melville Herskovits. Approving from the sidelines, Professor Robert Redfield sat in the front row of the select audience. It was a fascinating evening and got an enthusiastic write-up in the June 5, 1936 *Chicago Daily News*.

That August Katherine Dunham graduated from the University of Chicago with a bachelor's degree in social anthropology. Soon after, she was granted a Rockefeller Foundation fellowship to finance further studies towards her master's degree, to be taken under Dr. Herskovits.

During Katherine's absence from Chicago her dancing group had been kept alive by Ludmila Speranzeva and other friends. Reunited with them, Katherine promptly plunged into rehearsals. She had received a letter from the Young Men's Hebrew Association in Manhattan inviting her troupe to take part in a March 7, 1937 program titled "Negro Dance Evening." Though the YMHA auditorium was not an important theatre, this would be the Dunham company's first chance to appear before a New York audience—and New York was the center of dance in the United States. The invitation was promptly accepted.

Long before dawn on a blustery winter morning, Katherine and eight of her company started off on the long road to New York. They traveled in two old autos packed with their costumes and musical instruments, struggling through snow and winds for fifteen hours. Arriving at the YMHA they had barely enough time to change into their costumes before going on stage.

A magnificent male dancer named Archie Savage appeared in the act just before them. His musical accompanist was a sturdy, middle-aged Haitian named Papa Augustin. As Katherine heard the familiar Haitian drum rhythms, their association with the beautiful island made tears come to her eyes.

When their turn came the Dunham company performed modern ballet, as well as doing Haitian dances choreographed by Katherine for the occasion. She had heard about the wide-ranging taste of the New York audience who had a reputation for being hard to please. They obviously liked this evening's entertainment. The auditorium was filled with a buzz of approval as the audience buttoned up their coats to go home.

Backstage, jubilant at having captivated such a critical crowd, the dancers were in a mood to celebrate with a party. Handsome, jovial Archie Savage in-

vited the Dunham company to his mother's apartment in Harlem.

Helped by the women, Archie's mother prepared
a feast of pig's feet, neckbones, black-eyed peas, col-
lard greens, red beans, and rice—the first time Katherine ever ate "soul food." Then everyone sang and
danced, with Papa Augustin pounding the drum and
Katherine playing the boula. Towards morning they
stretched out to sleep in any available space—on the
floor, and even on a board stretched over the bath-
tub. During the long drive back to Chicago the next
day they slept some more.

Her ambitions rekindled by this taste of success—
for their performance was well-liked by the critics—
Katherine became restless. She thought the recent
Rockefeller fellowship money could be better applied
if it paid for a trip to Europe where she could see
other types of dancing and enlarge her knowledge of
the world. She decided to ask them to do this. Dr.
Herskovits begged her not to shift plans in mid-
stream. He said that having won Rockefeller support,
she should stay with it for the studies they had agreed
to finance.

In May the Rockefeller General Education Board
turned down Katherine's proposal for a trip to Europe. Making a cautious compromise, Katherine suspended her fellowship in June, saying she might take
it up again in October. She then applied for, and
was granted, a Guggenheim fellowship to pursue her
dance studies. One afternoon she dropped by to visit

Dr. Robert Redfield in his University of Chicago office. Redfield, long one of her favorite teachers, was a "homely-handsome" man with a craggy face, dry wit, and warm personality. This afternoon he leaned back in his chair in the office of the department of anthropology and asked what was troubling her.

Katherine told him of her conflict between becoming a teacher of anthropology or making a career in the dance world.

"This won't do," he said. "You must make up your mind immediately where your true loyalties belong."

Speaking passionately, Katherine let down her guard and told him everything she felt. Dr. Redfield suddenly looked up and smiled. "What's wrong with being a dancer?" he wanted to know.

Because Dr. Redfield had seen Katherine dance several times and admired her skill as a performer and choreographer, Katherine had known she could count on his sympathetic understanding. What she hadn't expected was immediate freedom. This was what she felt he had given her. If she didn't go into teaching she was afraid that everyone would think she'd misused the money given her by the Rosenwald and Rockefeller foundations. Dr. Redfield was releasing her from any sense of guilt about that, and telling her she had the right to do what she wanted.

A telephone call to Dr. Herskovits at Northwestern University followed. Nervously stammering over her words in an airless telephone booth Katherine

repeated much of what she had already told Dr. Redfield. There was a long silence at the other end.
Wondering if the line had gone dead, Katherine repeated her story again and finally Dr. Herskovits
acknowledged hearing what she said. There was no
doubt he was greatly disappointed in her decision.

For Katherine, however, there was no going back.
She got a job as Dance Director of the Federal Theatre Project in Chicago. This was one of the government's important programs for the arts during the
Depression, under the auspices of the Works Progress Administration. Their opening recital, *Ballet
Fedre*, was put on at Chicago's Great Northern Theatre on January 27, 1938. The next morning's newspapers praised the entire bill as "fine ballet" but they
raved about "a fiery folk ballet with choreography
by Katherine Dunham." They said *L'Ag'Ya* was
"danced with enough abandon to make some of the
preceding events seem pallid by comparison."

Katherine was at last hitting her stride. All the ele-
ments for success had long been there but this was
the first time she put them together to make an artistic whole. The Chauve Souris teachings of Ludmila Speranzeva, with their emphasis on acting and
story line as well as dancing skill, were an important
background influence. So was Ruth Page's ballet, *La
Guiablesse* in which Katherine had danced. This
had inspired her as an example of how folklore could
be worked into dance drama. Finally, there was Katherine's own field work in Martinique where she had

seen the fighting dance, Ag'Ya, heard the stories of Zombie activities, and used her imagination to create a story for the stage.

Critics clearly recognized the "authentic atmosphere of primitive rite" that *L'Ag'Ya* contained. From the ominous drumming in the Zombie scene to the sinuous love dance of Lalouse in the final act, the audience knew they were seeing something different from anything they'd witnessed before. *L'Ag'Ya* clearly stole the show," said the newspaper reviewers.

The same Chicago critics also praised the man who had designed the show's costumes and sets. They wrote, "John Pratt's handsome tropical costumes . . . shared the distinction of Miss Dunham's choreography." The team of John Pratt and Katherine Dunham, working together for the first time in this 1938 Federal Dance Project presentation of *L'Ag'Ya*, was eventually to become world famous.

Canadian-born John Pratt was then twenty-four years old, a very tall and handsome white man who had recently become part of the Dunham troupe. While an undergraduate at the University of Chicago, he had designed sets and costumes for their annual operettas. As an aspiring artist, he had seen his work exhibited at a Chicago downtown gallery as well as at university shows. He then got a job with the W.P.A. dance project which Katherine was directing. She greatly appreciated John Pratt's knowledge of how to design beautiful costumes in which a dancer could actually move without splitting the seams. She valued his artistic ability and his sense of style that helped so much in pulling a show together.

As late as March, 1938 the name of Katherine's husband, Jordis McCoo, was printed on a Sunday dance program as one of the members of her troupe. After that his name vanished and there is no doubt that he was rapidly disappearing out of Katherine's life. If there were no other reason, Jordis McCoo's postal job would keep him in Chicago while the Dunham Dance Company went on tour.

Under new, professional management the Dunham dancers were paid for giving performances in towns and cities throughout Illinois. One of their appearances was for a scholarship benefit in Katherine's hometown of Joliet, a contact made by Katherine's father. The local high school auditorium was sold out for the occasion, and the Dunham troupe received $332.50 for their dancing. They were all entertained afterwards at the home of Katherine's parents.

A touring company is a world of its own. Each member knows that he can't settle down to regular hours, a steady income, or a permanent place to live. Members of the troupe become close friends since they are together most of the time and share a dedication to their work. More than a year of this kind of close association strengthened the ties that were growing between Katherine Dunham and John Pratt, and led to their decision to get married.

Soon after Katherine received her divorce from

Jordis McCoo, she married John Pratt in a private ceremony on July 10, 1939 in Tecade, Mexico. Though Katherine was black and her husband white, their friends appreciated the close community of interests that bound the two together. Differences of color, religion, or nationality hardly matter in the world of artists where John and Katherine moved. Their friends felt their marriage chances were as good as—or better than—anyone else's.

Later that year Louis Schaeffer of the New York Labor Stage, who had seen Dunham and her dancers perform at the uptown YMHA, gave Katherine a chance to come to New York. He offered her the position of dance director to *Pins and Needles*, a successful Labor Stage show. Katherine accepted, making plans in her head. Saving the salary she earned, she intended to hire a theater where she could present a show of her own by the Dunham dance group.

It wasn't easy to find an empty stage in the middle of New York's busy winter theatrical season. Louis Schaeffer offered to help with that and with the necessary publicity. They found that the Windsor Theatre, on West 48th Street just off Broadway, was available on Sundays. There, the second Sunday in February, 1940, the Katherine Dunham Dance Company opened with Katherine's own *Tropics and Le Jazz Hot*. Included among the cast were her New York friends, Papa Augustin and Archie Savage.

The show was an immediate, sensational success.

"Katherine Dunham flared into unsuspecting New York last night like a comet. Unknown before her debut, she is today one of the most talked-about dancers" said one critic. Another noted that "Everybody in the audience beams with delight." John Pratt's costumes were commended for dressing the dancers in plumage "as brightly colored as tropical birds."

Among the collection of dances in *Tropics and Le Jazz Hot* was one that became a perennial favorite with audiences. Titled "Shore Excursion" and later called "Tropics," the dance opens with Katherine getting off a boat in Panama, carrying a bird cage and other baggage, and smoking an outrageously large cigar. Onlooking customers at Sloppy Joe's Bar are astonished at her appearance and the dance tells the story of their reactions to one another. Another dance, the "Florida Swamp Shimmy," was greatly admired by most dance critics but a few made prudish comments about its hip-swinging movements. Katherine, who had danced it, was gently tolerant in reply to their objections. She pointed out, "African movement is pelvic movement . . . just as movement in the neck, arms and upper torso is East Indian. It is natural and unselfconscious to the blacks . . ."

But such implied criticisms were rare. The majority of critics highly approved Katherine's "taste, research and talent." They had the perception to realize what she was trying to do. John Martin of *The New York Times* proclaimed, "With the arrival of

Katherine Dunham on the scene the development of a substantial Negro dance art begins to look decidedly bright. Her performance with her group at the Windsor Theatre may very well become a historic occasion, for certainly never before in all the efforts of recent years to establish the Negro dance as a serious medium has there been so convincing and authoritative an approach."

These were sweet words to Katherine's ears. Sweet, too, the continuing thunder of applause for many successive Sundays at the Windsor Theatre. And then came an offer for the Dunham Dance Company to take part in an all-Negro musical drama called *Cabin in the Sky*, due to open in the fall. The salary of almost three thousand dollars weekly was more than the Dunham Company had ever earned before, or ever dreamed of earning.

In her role as Georgia Brown, Katherine had her first chance to sing and act, as well as dance. Her performance—and the musical as a whole—was warmly acclaimed by the critics when the show opened at the Martin Beck Theatre in September, 1940. *Cabin in the Sky* enjoyed a long run.

During the course of it Katherine took time off to address the Anthropology Club of Yale University Graduate School, as well as the Anthropology Department of New York University. Using ten of her dancers, she illustrated the difference between East Indian and West Indian dancing. She also wrote and sold two articles about Martinique folk ways to the prestigous *Esquire* Magazine under the name of Kaye Dunn. Newspaper and magazine writers clamored to interview this intelligent and talented woman who didn't hesitate to speak her mind.

One of these interviewers was astonished when he heard her say she didn't really think she danced exceptionally well as a soloist. "My foot work is unremarkable," she pointed out.

Those nights she had spent lying on the damp Haitian ground during Voodoo initiation had revealed aches that she learned were arthritic. This kept her from being as fluid or quick as she would like. But neither the critics nor the audience were aware of any such limitations because she could suggest so much with a few movements.

She confessed something else to the interviewer. "I would like someday to live in Haiti for maybe four or five months of every year."

"What would you do there?" she was asked.

"My troupe and I could rest and rehearse between shows. We might start a dancing school in Port-au-Prince. All the Haitian children could come free. No one would ever be cold."

In the West Indies Katherine had discovered how well she felt away from the teeth-chattering winters of Chicago or New York. What better place could there be to escape the frigid weather and occasional chilly rebuffs than the warm social and geographical climate of Haiti as she had come to know it?

If she had any lingering doubts about her choice

of career, the stamp of approval was given in a letter written by Dr. Melville Herskovits. He said, "I think you were very wise to concentrate on your dancing and while it may have been nice to have you here I feel you are taking by far the better course."

*Fanny June Taylor Dunham,
with her son Albert Jr.*

Albert Dunham Sr.

Katherine Dunham as a child.

Annette Poindexter.

Albert Dunham Jr.
in high school.

Cécile, Doc, Fred Allsop, and Katherine Dunham in Haiti, 1936.

Katherine Dunham and John Pratt in Los Angeles, around 1942.

Katherine Dunham and Vanoye Aikens in L'Ag'Ya.

A scene from Stormy Weather, *starring Lena Horne, Bill Robinson, and Cab Calloway, with Katherine Dunham and her troupe.*

Katherine Dunham in her dressing room at
the LaFayette Theatre, Detroit, 1946.

Katherine Dunham and Maurice Chevalier, around 1949.

*Members of the Dunham Dance Company at a party
given by Katherine in Paris, 1950.*

Katherine Dunham, John Pratt, and their daughter Marie Christine, arriving at the Rome airport in 1953.

Lenwood Morris, Katherine
Dunham, Vanoye Aikens, and
Ricardo Avalez in Paris, 1954.

Katherine Dunham,
around 1955.

Katherine Dunham and Marie Christine in Australia, 1956.

III Ventures into the Unknown

9

Battles Against Prejudice

Cabin in the Sky stayed on Broadway until March, 1941, and then traveled across the continent to California where it closed in San Francisco. The Dunham Dance Company then toured the western night club circuit before settling in Hollywood to make several pictures.

Warner Brothers devoted an entire technicolor short, titled *Carnival of Rhythm*, to recording the dancing of the Dunham group. Katherine's troupe also did the dance interludes in *Star Spangled Rhythm* and *Pardon My Sarong*, both choreographed by Katherine.

She was fairly happy in California. Able to rent a large house facing the Pacific Ocean, she used the beach as a playground where her dancers could relax or rehearse. At the end of a hard day's work Katherine liked to take long walks along the shore, to be refreshed by the clean sea air and crashing sound of the waves. Later she rented the garden house of an estate that was near Ciro's night club, where she was often to perform in years to come.

But in letters home to her parents she complained about social slights she suffered from the Hollywood colony. The custom practiced in the snobbish star system of the time was that the biggest stars talked only to one another, seldom mingling with actors or actresses of less importance. Katherine thought she also detected color prejudice as a cause for exclusion.

After their Hollywood stay, when Katherine took a new show of her own on a national tour, the existence of racial prejudice became more obvious. When *Tropical Review,* managed by international impressario Sol Hurok, arrived at cities or towns to give their performance, the dancers often had to trek wearily from hotel to boarding house looking for rooms where they could stay. It was just as hard to find a restaurant that would accept blacks.

In Cincinnati Katherine filed suit against the Netherlands Plaza for refusing to accommodate her. After a court battle, she won admission to the hotel for herself and any other black who wanted a room there. She also successfully sued Chicago's Blackstone Hotel. In the border state of Kentucky she steeled herself for a direct confrontation. She had noticed blacks in the audience being restricted to the balcony of Louisville's Municipal Auditorium. So, after bowing to the audience's applause at the end of the show she straightened up to say a few well-chosen words:

"Friends, we are glad to have made you happy. This is the last time we shall play Louisville because the management refuses to let people like us sit by people like you. Maybe after the war we shall have democracy and I can return. Until then God bless you for you will need it."

Though her voice was soft, her message came across like a clap of thunder. The audience was stunned. There was a burst of applause. Then many people, some with tears in their eyes, went backstage to talk to her about what she had said. One woman remarked, "You shouldn't have done that. It was like getting a slap in the face."

"How do you think we feel?" Katherine wondered. She told something of those feelings later to a New York reporter. "The terrific beating the Negro takes must end. Sometimes you think anything would be better than this. You feel you're going to break under the strain. I work with the purpose of reducing the pressure on the Negro performer. In helping him to work with a free mind and without stress you help all the Negro people."

One city singled out by Katherine for its hospitality and racial tolerance was San Francisco, which she said "stood out like a shining light." She said the

Mark Hopkins Hotel had given her a beautiful three-room suite and that she and members of her company were able to eat wherever they wanted in the city. Otherwise the national record regarding racial discrimination was not good. And by this time, Katherine said, "I am getting good and mad about it because of the war."

America was by then involved in World War II, and its people, supposedly fighting against tyranny and bigotry abroad, were often practicing it themselves at home. "It would seem ridiculous if it were not so tragic," Katherine said.

By then John Pratt had been drafted into the army. Stationed as a private at Fort Eustis, Virginia, he was waiting to go overseas. This meant it was up to Katherine to manage the designing, sets, and stage production, as well as all the other company business, without her husband's help.

And the company itself was quite a handful. She told one reporter, "It is like taking care of a large family . . . worse, because children go off to school" whereas Katherine's dancers were constantly with her. She worried even more when they were off somewhere, concerned about what kind of mischief their high spirits might get them into.

Keeping them busy was the best antidote to this. On their 1943–44 tour throughout the United States and Canada, Katherine constantly varied the show's pace and made other revisions. This kept her dancers from being bored and the show from going stale. Rehearsals were held daily. Sometimes Katherine added a new number to try out fresh ideas, reworked an old number to improve it, or dropped a piece she felt lacked audience appeal.

A new and exciting number introduced in *Tropical Review* was "Rites de Passage." Its theme was the puberty, fertility, and mating rituals of Africa. One part of the story told in dance is of a boy being initiated into manhood. New York dance critic Walter Terry said he liked the way it caught "the sense of loneliness, the terror, the challenge, the testing, and the acceptance." John Martin of *The New York Times* said, "Its movement is markedly uninhibited and certainly it is nothing to take Grandma to see, but it is an excellent piece of work." However Boston authorities were shocked by its boldness and censored the dance. Neither Boston's critics nor audience agreed with the authorities' judgment.

Still, it must have been a relief for Katherine and her company to return to New York's more tolerant atmosphere at the end of the show's run, to be told, "The company is as lively and graceful as ever, and Miss Dunham in the full bloom of her successful beauty and showmanship is a stunning entertainer."

But Katherine never rested on her laurels. She told an interviewer: "The time between productions can be the most creative period for a permanent company such as mine." To keep her dancers working, choreographic ideas flowing, and some money coming in, she decided to open a school of dance in New

York. This would be an excellent way to train new dancers to replace members of her company who might leave for any reason. It would also enable her to pass on the Dunham techniques and rounded view of life to younger generations.

For as Katherine developed her plan she built on an idea that had worked well for the Denishawn School founded in 1920 in Los Angeles by two gifted dancers, Ted Shawn and his wife Ruth St. Denis. In their school they taught dancing in connection with other related arts and philosophies. Only with such a background could an artist hope to make an important, original statement of his own in the world, they believed. And they had been remarkably successful, turning out such stellar dancer-choreographers as Martha Graham, Doris Humphrey, and Charles Weidman.

Going beyond the Denishawn School idea, Katherine had notions of her own. Having mixed blood in her own veins, she wanted to encourage worldwide tolerance and understanding. Racial restrictions, she felt, were like walls shutting people off from the richness of multi-cultural exchange. Her school was to be her way of trying to blast through those walls.

Katherine first hired the former studio of famous dancer Isadora Duncan in Caravan Hall to serve as school headquarters. It turned out to be too small. In late 1945 Lee Shubert gave her a gift of three years' free rent for the entire top floor of an old theatre he owned at 220 West 43rd Street, just off

Broadway. Twelve pupils enrolled the first week. Less than a year later 420 students had signed up. They came from such far-away places as Switzerland, Palestine, Ireland, and the French island possessions. Eventually former soldiers came by benefit of the United States Veterans' Educational Bill of Rights.

About 20 percent to 30 percent of her students were white, and almost half were young children. If some young people showed promise but couldn't pay tuition Katherine gave them working scholarships. In return for helping to wash and mend costumes, keeping the building clean, or running the elevator, they could take any courses they wanted, free of charge. This cut in on profits, but dollars weren't primarily what the school was about.

The courses offered at the Katherine Dunham School of Dance were esthetics, classical drama, speech, philosophy, anthropology, theatrical production and staging, radio technique, makeup, and French, Spanish, and Russian languages. Classes were also given in ballet, modern dance, Dunham technique, tap, social dancing, percussion, visual design, and body movement for actors.

The school was a fascinating place to visit. In the wardrobe room, students sprawled on the big sewing tables while instructors gave lecture-demonstrations and everyone waited for wrenched zippers or ripped seams to be mended. In another room was Papa Henri Augustin, picturesquely dressed in bright blue blouse, denim pants, and straw hat, giving classes in percussion. His students included middle-aged housewives, businessmen, and small children.

When Katherine wasn't illustrating steps in the Dunham technique she often dropped in on Papa's other class in creole songs. Sitting on the floor she would hold one bare foot in her lap while her soft voice mingled with Papa's husky tones and the children's sweet trebles chanting the West Indian music she knew and loved.

Besides his teaching duties, Papa served as chief drummer to the Dunham company and Katherine's consultant on Haitian folklore. He was also a close, sympathetic friend and Katherine needed such support. She had never really had this sort of rapport with her family, she felt. Her triumphs in the theatre, impressive to everybody else, had not been totally acceptable to her rather strait-laced stepmother or father. They were somewhat embarrassed reading the Joliet newspaper reprints of New York reviews that said Katherine's performances "made the stage fairly sizzle." And even before Albert became ill, he was probably too introverted to be really attuned to her lively, public life. Katherine had a thoughtful side to her own personality, too, though—the side that studied the folk cultures on which her dances were based, masterminded the school, or quietly sat at a desk to write articles and books. In early 1946 she was working on a slim volume about her anthropological visit to Jamaica, titled *Journey to Accom-*

pong, to be published by Henry Holt the following year.

Katherine knew that both writing and school activities would be highly approved by her family. Unfortunately, neither paid enough money to support her chief interest, the Dunham Dance Company and their work. She sought other opportunities to build their finances. In 1945 Katherine choreographed dance numbers for another all-Negro musical titled *Carib Song,* which was not a Broadway success. Another show she choreographed was Philip Yordan's *Windy City,* which received mixed reviews. The Dunham company also cut records for a Decca album on West Indian music, did an hour spectacular on television, and filled night club engagements.

Then they began rehearsing for another show of their own. John Pratt was out of the army at last, in time to plan the sets and costumes. *Bal Negre's* outstanding new number was carried from *Carib Song* because Katherine rightly judged it too good to die with that short-lived production. "Shango," based on Katherine's field experiences, featured a youth whose religious frenzy makes him believe he is possessed by a snake. As the dancer imitates the snake's crawling and climbing abilities his body becomes remarkably fluid—a sight which, combined with the drumming accompaniment and menacing jungle atmosphere, caused "Shango" to be a favorite of audiences everywhere.

Bal Negre opened at the Belasco Theatre in November, 1946. The next morning's reviews said the show was "brightly staged and brilliantly costumed by John Pratt" and was "an arresting, frequently exciting review." They remarked that the "usually staid stage was alive with glistening, pulsating bodies . . . finest primitive dancing." While recognizing that its "pattern follows pretty closely that of tropical reviews of other seasons . . . a kind of cross section of Caribbean and North American Negro folk culture cast in theatrical form," they said this one "surpasses its predecessors to be far and away the best of the Dunham shows to date."

It was enormously satisfying for Katherine to see *Bal Negre*, which represented everything she believed in, receive such praise. The genius of black dance was to get even wider exposure in the future. For the first time the Katherine Dunham Dance Company was going abroad, booked to perform before international audiences in Mexico, Europe, and South America.

10

Public Success, Private Tragedy

*I*n Mexico and in Europe, Katherine Dunham was treated like a queen. Those first exciting years abroad, from 1947 through 1949, were perhaps an unequaled high point in Katherine's life and career. Everywhere she went, adulation and hospitality were heaped upon her, and the company basked in glowing reviews. But as always in the theatre, there was a side of the coin unseen by the audience—weariness caused by constant traveling, problems with her dancers, and the difficulties, financial and other, of transporting a large company of people and tons of baggage.

Arriving at their first stop on the tour, Mexico City, the company discovered that their luggage was still in transit. The Esperanza Iris Theatre had been sold out; the audience could not be disappointed. So, without scenery or costumes, the dancers went on-stage in their rehearsal clothes and performed against a plain backdrop. Their vigor and style supplied its own vibrancy, and the cheering audience expressed their appreciation of the show and of this gallant spirit of improvisation. A few days later their baggage caught up with them, and others swarmed to see the completely dressed show.

"La Katerina," as the people affectionately nicknamed her, was personally invited to meet Miguel Alemán, President of Mexico, at his request. Leading Mexican artists and intellectuals like Diego Rivera, José Orozco, and Carlos Chávez deluged Katherine and her company with dinner invitations. The younger members of the diplomatic corps also gave a series of parties.

Practicing a charming brand of diplomacy herself, Katherine expressed her troupe's happiness and her own at being so warmly welcomed into Mexico. She hoped their dancing was more than entertainment. "Anything that helps explain one group of human beings to another will tend to dissipate misunderstandings, fears and prejudices," she said.

Katherine was asked to give an anthropological lecture at the Palacio de Bellas Artes, and was otherwise so much in demand that her reservations to move on to Acapulco had to be cancelled many times. U.S. newspapers reported to their readers, "La Katerina has certainly rung the bell south of the border."

In New York, the picture was less bright. Katherine learned that registration had gone down at her dance school. After a promising beginning, the school had been put under a Board of Directors in mid-1947 and given a charter from New York State as the Katherine Dunham School of Cultural Arts Inc. Perhaps owing to new state qualifications, perhaps to the absence of Katherine's magical presence, there was a subsequent drop in student enrollment. Katherine had to forward money earned from their performances to keep the school going—the first of many times this was to happen.

"It is the old story of great artists—success and financial chaos," she wrote a friend in San Francisco. "Somehow in life there ought to be a way around."

When Katherine and her dance company finally tore themselves away from Mexico City, the farewell party given them overflowed with champagne and distinguished, devoted patrons of the dance. They then left for a successful tour of the provinces. Their stay in Mexico, originally set for a few weeks' engagement, stretched out to last over five months.

In London the following year, the company opened with their new *Caribbean Rhapsody*, at the Prince of Wales Theatre on June 2nd. Their performances were sellouts. One newspaper writer said Katherine had "stolen the heart of London." Another said the Dunham company's impact was similar to the arrival of the immortal Diaghilev Ballet early in the century. In a word, stunning. In October Katherine was invited to address the Royal Anthropological Society, and was made an honorary member.

When the Dunham Dance Company moved on to Paris, their successes were repeated. Katherine was hailed as "the most extravagantly successful American dancer since Josephine Baker." Paris spring fashions included the "Dunham line" inspired by Katherine's bold show personality and her husband's vivid sense of color and costuming. A sculptor modeled Dunham's feet and had them cast in bronze to be displayed in a new French museum of important personalities. She had a duplicate made for a museum in Haiti. Painter André Quellier of Rue Blanche sketched and painted Katherine and her company as they rehearsed.

Paris has always been a favorite of Americans, and it was at its best in the mild summer of 1948. Katherine and John Pratt and the rest of the Dunham company were not in Europe only to work. They went as tourists too, as eager to explore as any other travelers visiting a foreign country for the first time. They enjoyed walking along the Seine River, buying from the flower shops and bookstalls, watching artists at work, the fishermen, and children at play. At night they watched the excursion boats cruising the Seine and the lights from the river bridges reflected in the water, giving the city the look of a fairyland.

A collection of some of the world's greatest works of art awaited them when they visited the Louvre Museum. Tucked all over Paris were the wonderful little cafés that made dining out even in ordinary restaurants a delight. When they were not performing or at rehearsals they could enjoy themselves as private people.

As public personalities they had different advantages. International celebrities wanted to meet them and offered a lively social life. Newspaper pictures taken during this period show Katherine and John Pratt and members of their company exchanging toasts over dinner or at parties with such notables as the poet and artist Jean Cocteau, the dancers Josephine Baker and Mistinguette, the American tobacco heiress Doris Duke, actors and actresses Maurice Chevalier, Orson Welles, and Jennifer Jones, and producer David Selznick. Life was made richer, easier, and more entertaining in many ways.

But as public personalities they were also exposed to the sometimes overzealous attention of their fans and admirers. To escape this and retain a measure of privacy, Katherine and John moved to a hotel in the Paris suburbs. Katherine took up painting because she wanted "to do something to help me hang onto the French scenery. It is so beautiful." She added, "It is nice to be liked—but in Paris the people devour you!"

Adulation was not confined to the star of the Dunham troupe. Katherine took several students from

the Dunham dance school on the tour. One of them was Eartha Kitt, who had studied French, Spanish, and body movement for actors, as well as dance, because she wanted to "have more to offer than a pretty face and a nice voice." Lured by Paris nightclubs, she deserted the troupe to start a sensational, highly paid career of her own as a singer.

Eartha Kitt was not the only member of the company to drop out. Talley Beatty, one of the original Dunham dance group that performed at the YMHA, took off to establish a company of his own. So, eventually, did Jean-Léon Destiné, the one who'd danced possession by a snake in "Shango," and Bobby Capo who later became a South American singing star.

Having watched these members of her company develop into stage personalities under her tutelage, Katherine found it hard to let them go. Others left for different reasons. Katherine ruefully wrote a friend, "The country is very beautiful . . . the company in high spirits. We can't all help but feel a little sad, however, that Othello is going to be married in October. Then it is only a question of wondering how long before she, like Ritchie, will be off to housekeeping. It is a question with me how many of these well-groomed young ladies will leave Europe!"

Sickness also took its toll, and Katherine counted on her New York school to send other dancers to fill these gaps. That had not turned out to be as reliable as she had hoped. Other dance companies were raiding her school for talent, and Katherine had to warn the school head, "Be sure to see that all the scholarship students have signed their agreements" giving first job consideration to the Dunham Dance Company that had trained them.

Financial difficulties plagued them. Katherine had to support her company for weeks between performances, and pay their transportation to the next engagement. There were special taxes and fees to pay and problems in that they were only permitted to take a limited amount of cash out of a country. This was sometimes not enough to support them in the next place.

Some of the dancers liked to live expensively. They had to be warned that they could expect no more salary advances or raises and must live within their means. Katherine observed that there were those "who are at present living on half of what they did before and are enjoying it and it is only a matter of wishing to do so . . . All of us have had our lessons in extravagance and plan [to pay] our debts and . . . put some money aside."

Many members of the company took this advice to heart. A few, however, sulked and skipped rehearsals or performances. To maintain company discipline, Katherine levied fines for "tardiness of any description and misconduct in the execution of theatrical performance obligations." This money was set aside in a special fund to be paid out to company members "during periods of genuine illness."

A friend from the United States wrote Katherine admiringly, "I think the miracle of the loaves and fishes is child's play compared to what you are managing to do."

The company traveled on through France, Germany, Holland, Italy, and into the Scandinavian countries. There things got off to a bad start. On a Stockholm stage, as Katherine came out for her famous "Woman With the Cigar" number, she saw the King and his party in the Royal Box. Burdened with props in each hand and a birdcage on her head, all she could do was put some extra zip into her performance to honor them. She was later roundly scolded by her local agent who said it was disrespectful not to bow to the King before continuing her number.

Also, an indignant man wrote a letter to the Swedish newspapers criticizing *L'Ag'Ya* as "the most unconcealed erotic exhibition ever performed" and demanding it be taken out of the Dunham show. Such a reaction might be expected in puritanical Boston, but came as a surprise in liberal Stockholm. Besides, the cost of living was high there. And they were out of bookings for four weeks, which "threw everybody into quite a panic."

It was a hard fight to keep everything going, to keep it all glued together and working right, and Katherine was worn out by the struggle. She found herself "drinking just about every evening during the show" and complained that hers was "a miserable existence, full of discouragement, doubt, anxiety."

All these troubles, however, seemed insignificant next to the shock of her brother's death. Albert Millard Dunham Jr. died at St. Elizabeth's hospital in May, 1949. What made the news most bitter was the fact that it happened "just as his recovery was practically 100%" as she confided to a friend in a grief-stricken letter. In a few weeks he would have left to resume life outside the hospital. Now she was devastated by the realization that all Albert's "goodness and intellectual brilliance" were forever quenched.

Years afterward she still recalled her brother's illness and death as "the supreme tragedy" of her life. She became sick from being so depressed and overtired. Her New York physician prescribed injections of vitamins and hormones which he sent. Katherine made an appointment to see him on a brief trip she would make back to the United States to console her parents. "I dread to feel in such complete exhaustion," she said.

At such a time Katherine also needed to consult her friend, psychoanalyst Erich Fromm, whose warm and wise understanding "saved my life many a time," she said. It may have been at his urging that she decided to find a place where she could establish some kind of permanent base. She badly needed a retreat where she could recoup her energies. John Pratt and the rest of the company were just as frazzled. She declared "This year I have promised myself definitely some sort of *pied-à-terre*—perhaps in Mexico. It seems so safe and friendly and solid."

But Mexico was not to be the place she would choose for her haven. Her old friend, Dumarsais Estimé, now President of Haiti, had invited her to the 1949 Bicentenary Exposition there. Katherine decided to go, taking along her school's revered drumming instructor, Papa Henri Augustin. Knowing he yearned to see his own country again, she wanted to repay him for "the glamor and truth which he brought to the Dunham School from which I was all too frequently absent."

Katherine, too, was glad to return to the sparkling bay of Port-au-Prince, to the blue water "so transparent one had the impression of being able to count the scales on the striped and coral and blue fish that streaked through it." In retrospect her student days there seemed to have been an idyllic time.

For her achievements as a dancer, and for always having presented the controversial country of Haiti "in the best light before the rest of the world," President Dumarsais Estimé pinned a beribboned decoration on Katherine's breast that made her a Chevalier in the Haitian Legion of Honor. As they shook hands, Katherine noticed that Estimé's felt cold. More unsmiling than ever, he seemed heavily burdened by his office, the accomplishments of which Katherine could see as she was personally escorted from one end of the island to the other by the Minister of Tourism and Culture. The exposition itself was a major achievement, but Katherine also saw slums torn down to make way for decent housing, and heard about Estimé's attempt to enact social security legislation in the face of stubborn opposition. Katherine was aware that "social reform where there is no middle class and where there is absentee ownership is hard to bring about." She sympathized with the loneliness of Estimé's mission.

After a round of parties and receptions, Katherine returned to Europe in August to finish the season's trouping. Talking things over with her husband, she decided to have a friend inquire about the possibility of purchasing the crumbling remains of the haunted Habitation Leclerc.

As the year closed, she heard about her father's death. Then came news that President Dumarsais Estimé had been forced to resign and been exiled from Haiti. In a few years Haiti was to undergo tremendous political changes that would eventually affect even the small haven of Habitation Leclerc.

11

At Home in Haiti

*B*ack in America, performing in *Caribbean Rhapsody* at the Broadway Theatre in April, 1950, the Dunham company was hailed by the critics as having "new chic." They said, "Playing in Europe has given the company a sense of being exotic . . . The new Miss Dunham is an assured and lovely artist, possessed of an aristocratic languor which is quite irresistible . . . The costumes by John Pratt contribute one of the most constantly rewarding aspects of Miss Dunham's production." The consensus was, "Paris has done wonders" for the whole company.

The shadow of racial prejudice still haunted Katherine, however. "In Europe we felt so loved," she told a reviewer. "I think the saddest thing in American history is her people returning here and not feeling they are coming home."

Certainly Katherine did not expect to be discriminated against in South America, a continent where black blood is shared by so many, from mansion to ghetto.

But in Brazil, at the start of their South American tour, they were refused accommodations at São Paulo's Hotel Esplanada. Indignant at such treatment, Katherine again sued the hotel management as she had in the Midwest years before. As the news spread about what had happened many South Americans were equally scandalized by the hotel's actions. Newspapers joined in a general clamor to legislate a strict anti-discrimination law. As a result a bill was passed demanding penalties of three to twelve months imprisonment and up to ten thousand dollars in fines for any future acts of discrimination.

Katherine and her company had a happier experience in Argentina. President Juan Perón befriended them, and his wife, a former movie star named Evita, invited Katherine to go with her on inspection tours of schools, orphanages, and homes for unwed mothers and prostitutes. Señora Perón also asked Katherine to give a performance for the benefit of her numerous charities.

On the heels of the South American tour the Dunham company was booked to perform in Jamaica. They would then move to Haiti for six months' rest and rehearsal at Habitation Leclerc which Katherine had leased with an option to buy. Such were Katherine's plans. For over three years her dance company had been constantly on the move. It was high time to pause in their travels to get back a sense of themselves, and to work on a new show.

Katherine was blissfully looking forward to relaxing at Habitation Leclerc. She was not prepared for any complications beforehand. But she was to find two cherished, old-time Haitian friends in Jamaica. Fred Allsop was living there, the handsome young man who had been Katherine's close companion and heroic rescuer during her early anthropological escapades. Katherine learned that Fred had left his job at the Port-au-Prince garage to work for the naturalist Ivan Sanderson. On one of Sanderson's trips to Honduras, Fred met and married Colleen, a pretty young woman, and they now had two baby daughters.

"Eyeing each other with a natural antagonism," as Katherine described the scene of their first meeting, the two women gradually relaxed over cocktails and started to become good friends, while their husbands treated each other with a kind of hearty boyishness.

The news about another old friend was less happy. Ex-President Dumarsais Estimé was also in Kingston with his family at this time—a hunted man. He was having great trouble finding a house where he and his family could live. Jamaican landlords were afraid to have anything to do with them.

The root of Estimé's troubles was the Haitian people's love for him, and their continuing appreciation
of how he had tried to improve their life. The new
Haitian government, with former army officer Paul
Magloire as their President, feared that Estimé plot-
ted to rally the people's support for his return.

Merely knowing that Estimé stayed on the nearby
island of Jamaica caused Colonel Magloire and his
supporters to be uneasy. Jamaicans believed that Haitian secret agents would be sent to make an attempt
on Estimé's life. Any Jamaican landlord who accom-
modated the family put his property in danger. And
Fred Allsop warned Katherine that any person seen
in Estimé's company risked physical harm.

Still Katherine persisted in contacting this dear
friend. She finally caught up with the Estimés in a
Kingston suburb where they were temporarily being
sheltered. She thought the ex-President bore himself
with as much pride and dignity as ever, but he was
much thinner and his eyes looked haunted. Meeting
Estimé's wife for the first time, Katherine was "impressed by her beauty and calm under the circumstances." She gave the Estimés tickets to her show
and said she would try to help them find a more permanent place to stay.

But when Katherine asked her own motherly land-
lady to rent the Estimés a few of her rooms, the
woman angrily refused. Fred and Colleen Allsop
were equally determined not to get themselves or
their family mixed up in any political intrigue.

While arguing the case with the Allsops over dinner one night Katherine felt an excruciating stab of pain in her right side. She was rushed to a hospital to have an emergency appendicitis operation. During her convalescence she received cards and flowers from many people—but not a word from the Estimés.

Finally Fred grew sufficiently concerned about such a long silence to track down the Estimé family himself. He found them in time for Katherine to throw a luau lunch in their honor before she had to leave Jamaica. Planning the lunch carefully, Katherine prepared all the food herself and invited as guests only those people known to be sympathetic to the ex-President.

At the end of the lunch, Estimé asked to see Katherine alone. It was hard for him to ask a favor, he said, but his financial plight was drastic. If he could not get a letter to Haiti to release some of his money, or his wife's, they would be without means to pay their way. Would Katherine deliver such a letter when she traveled to Port-au-Prince? Estimé assured her that the letter had no political overtones. He said he now understood and accepted the fact that he would never again be given the chance to live in Haiti even as a private citizen.

Underneath Estimé's quiet admission Katherine sensed his heartbreak. Deeply moved, she said she would smuggle in such a letter for him, though "if it were intercepted the consequences for all of us would be something about which I did not care to speculate."

As the person least likely to be suspected of political sentiments or connections in a country she'd never seen before, Katherine's secretary agreed to carry the letter. She successfully passed it through customs hidden in her dress.

Katherine was understandably wary of how Colonel Magloire would receive her and her company when they reached Haiti. Not only was she known to be a dear friend of Estimé, she was frightened about smuggling in Estimé's letter. But when he met her, President Paul Magloire proved to be agreeable, personally charming, and openly admiring of Katherine's talents and accomplishments. To her surprise she found him "hard to resist" as he welcomed her and her entourage to Haiti.

About twenty-four people came with Katherine including fifteen dancers, some musicians, composers, business managers, secretaries, and others. Among them was Papa Henri Augustin. Another visitor soon expected was Katherine's widowed stepmother, Annette Poindexter Dunham. Katherine's new property was large enough to accommodate all of them, though only in a rudimentary way.

Despite its few comforts, there were many picturesque qualities to recommend Habitation Leclerc. Cannon balls lined the long driveway through impressive grounds, filled with exotic plants, shrubs, fountains, statues, staircases, and several pools. The main building was an old frame house thought to have been inhabited by Pauline Bonaparte Leclerc, and other stone and cement structures had formerly served as slave quarters, a cook house, a summer house, and a pavilion.

Moving into these makeshift quarters, the company set about arranging sleeping and cooking accommodations. One couple was too much in love to notice the disadvantages such as rainwater plopping from leaks in the roof, and the sight of large, tropical cockroaches parading out of cracks in the floor. Others, however, grumbled a little before they began choking on clouds of smoke that came from the faulty kitchen charcoal stove.

Sounds of coughing turned to screams of terror, as a snake, coiled peacefully on a rafter above their heads, was smoked out from his perch and started descending to the ground. Wilbert Bradley, one of the male dancers of the company, acted heroically. In Brazil he'd been attracted to a lady who appeared on stage with a snake. Now he copied her act so convincingly that the snake followed him out of doors as he led the way, dancing a samba. The women collapsed in partly hysterical laughter, and though calm was eventually restored no one slept very well that first night.

In the morning, to make things more liveable, they started cleaning up and putting rooms in order. "Pauline's Pool" named for its decorative bas relief showing Pauline Bonaparte Leclerc being served fruit by slaves as she lounged on a sofa, became a favorite gathering place. Here the dancers assembled to sun themselves, swim, gossip, and read letters or newspapers from home. Some of the women rehearsed there, one of them practicing her singing in such a powerfully deep contralto that Katherine thought she must be heard all the way down to Port-au-Prince. A ballet barre was improvised at the nearby pavilion.

They were hardly settled when the frequent command invitations from President Magloire and his wife began. Like Evita Perón, Madame Magloire headed many charities for which she asked Katherine's help. President Magloire was more interested in the discovery that the inhabitants of Habitation Leclerc always put on a great show.

He developed a voracious appetite for the company of Katherine Dunham and her troupe. Magloire's magnificently uniformed officers were often dispatched with demands for the group's presence at some splendid social affair. Just as frequently he sent helmeted gendarmes to make an announcement of his own shortly forthcoming visit.

Katherine had barely twelve hours notice to plan one memorable evening for the President. Set around Pauline's Pool were candle-lit tables where a feast was ready to be served. As President Magloire arrived with his wife in a flourish of guards, a hastily improvised band struck up the Haitian National Anthem. Magloire stood solemnly at attention. The band then swung into a Meringue and the President gallantly led his wife onto the floor to open the dancing.

Lucille Ellis, a long-time member of the Dunham company, served as one of the evening's charming hostesses. Lenwood Morris, who had run away from high school to join the troupe in 1941, put on a grand display of acrobatic diving. Vanoye Aikens, a minister's son who became Katherine's chief dancing partner in 1942, served as a kind of soothing social secretary to Annette Dunham who fussed about the proper seating protocol. Everyone else cooperated beautifully to make the event a great success.

Katherine's warm feeling of love for her aging stepmother was somewhat cooled by Annette's attitude of rigid respectability during this visit. Annette was not comfortable in such a totally foreign atmosphere. She missed her Joliet circle of friends, her church-going, and her TV programs.

Annette was not the only one who wouldn't be sorry to leave Habitation Leclerc. The members of the Dunham Dance Company were not as happy there as Katherine would have wished. In Haiti, among people of their own kind and color, the Dunham troupe no longer stood out. They'd been spoiled by attentions they received as uniquely exotic personalities in other countries of the world, and they missed that. Katherine couldn't interest them in the African roots of dance as preserved in the Haitian back country—a subject that fascinated her. Entertainment available in the town's bars or clubs was limited, and they were no longer amused by the com-

mand performances demanded by President Magloire.

Their boredom struck a blow at Katherine's dream
of making Habitation Leclerc the permanent headquarters for her company. Despite this disappointment, Katherine's own appreciation of Habitation
Leclerc grew stronger daily. Returning there after a
day's trip away she always felt "a thrill of anticipation, an expectancy always fulfilled of beauty, safety
and the love of the people" who served her there or
lived on her land.

But walking around the grounds late at night she
had to admit she felt a menace in the atmosphere—
a feeling of apprehension perhaps based on the treach-
eries of Haitian political life she had witnessed, or on
the knowledge of the blood spilled there during General Rochambeau's time.

Papa Augustin advised Katherine to have the place
exorcised of evil. And then something happened that
made up her mind to do this. John Pratt, returning
late from a visit to town, heard his mother-in-law
let out a piercing yell and he went to see what was
the matter. Everyone else heard the scream too, and
came running—including Katherine who had gone
to bed early with a fever.

Annette stood outside her doorway in her night-
gown, trembling with fright. A black man had come
onto her porch, she said. His chest was bare, his
hands tied behind his back, and he was crying and
pleading for help. When Annette screamed he ran

away and seemed to have disappeared in the vicinity of the old slave quarters.

With Papa Augustin's approval, Katherine sent for Kam. She was a seventy-year-old priestess, once a lady pirate, who had the bearing of a queen and a gift for prophecy and exorcising.

Exorcism has a long tradition in many religions. It is the chasing away of evil spirits from a place known to be haunted by them. At Habitation Leclerc, the source of evil was well known. Many stories had been told about the sadistic deeds of General Rochambeau who, on these grounds, had Haitian military men and slaves tortured, drowned, asphyxiated, fed to dogs, even buried alive. Katherine had proof of Rochambeau's actual residency at Leclerc. Among other mementos dug up on the property was a silver fork bearing the insignia of his regiment.

Before proceeding with her exorcisms Kam settled in for six days and nights to get the "feel" of the place. She would have to study the cause of the trouble before understanding the cleansing ceremonies required by the gods.

Seizing this time to steal away from her usual filial, professional, and other obligations, Katherine looked up some old Haitian friends. Inquiring about the two priestesses who had helped initiate her into Voodoo, Katherine learned that Téoline and Dégrasse were both dead. So was the innocent ten-year-old girl who had danced to Erzulie, Haitian equivalent of the Virgin Mary. A young boy who had been another fellow initiate had become a kind of con man making his living off unsuspecting tourists.

Doc Reeser, the American ex-Marine, had apparently been "possessed" by the libertine spirit of Haitian god Papa Guedé often enough to wreck his health. He returned home to his white wife and children in Florida. Before he left Haiti, Doc had given Cécile some things he knew she dearly wanted—a sewing machine and several gold teeth. Cécile was very sad without him but could not believe he would stay away. Her feelings about Doc's devotion to her proved correct. He eventually returned to spend his last days with the black woman in the country he loved most on earth.

For Katherine, Haiti would always be full of ghosts like these—and they were not malevolent. She awaited Kam's findings with composure. One evening, when the air was clear and everything washed to a shining freshness by a light rain, Katherine was called out of her bed. She followed Kam, walking with a sense of calmness and security she had not felt before. No special ceremony was involved, but there was no doubt that Kam's prayers and concentration had somehow cleared the threatening atmosphere and restored a sense of equanimity to Habitation Leclerc—at least for the present.

John Pratt agreed with Katherine that, regardless of how the members of the dance company felt about Habitation Leclerc, the two of them would go ahead with plans to enlarge and improve the property for their own enjoyment and possible later retirement.

But the Dunham dancers were glad when the time came to leave Haiti and go touring with another show. After a series of short bookings at western nightclubs they were going to return to Europe— this time for a longer stay.

12

More Tours Abroad

*T*hough it was on her first trip abroad that Katherine Dunham had met the noted art critic, Bernard Berenson, it was during her second European tour that their friendship blossomed. There were many points of resemblance between Berenson and Katherine's brother, Albert, and both men helped shape her future.

Berenson was small, and slender, like Albert, and had the same philosophical cast of mind. Albert, a black, and Berenson, a Lithuanian Jew, had both been subjected to some prejudice and discrimination. Both had an early determination to succeed in their chosen careers. But whereas Albert's promise had been cut off by illness and death, Berenson lived a long life as a renowned authority and writer on Italian Renaissance art.

A constant stream of artists, philosophers, students, statesmen, and writers came to Berenson's home, I Tatti, near Florence, Italy. Berenson's reputation as host and stimulating conversationalist was famous. An invitation to visit I Tatti was compared to seeing Michelangelo's "David" or the Roman Forum.

Katherine felt lucky when friends arranged for her to go there. The "command luncheon" date was set for a day that Katherine was busy with newspaper photographers. "No one ever keeps Berenson waiting," she was warned. Her friends were in a panic as she set off tardily for I Tatti. By the time she arrived Berenson was walking up and down in a perfect fury at his luncheon's delay.

Eighty-six years old then, in 1950, Berenson was still an attractive man. White haired, with a short, straight nose and a neatly trimmed Van Dyke beard, he habitually wore a red carnation in the buttonhole of his pale gray suits. His curiosity about people, books, and painting was still zestfully alive. To the end of his days he retained his appreciation of beauty in any form, especially beautiful women whose presence noticeably inspired his best flights of talk.

And on his first look at Katherine he was struck by her beauty. He admired the bold green and red check of her dress against the chocolate brown of her skin. He liked the way it draped her body rather than hung from it. He wrote in his diary that night,

"Katherine Dunham is herself a work of art, a fanciful arabesque in all her movements and a joy to the eye in colour." He said she looked "like an Egyptian queen, like Queen Ti . . ."

His anger over her late arrival soon forgotten, he was further impressed when they started to talk. He recorded her opinion that it was a pity the artist, in search for constant novelty to satisfy sated audiences, often "had to hurry and fuss and do anything sensational, being given no time to meditate and mature." He noted she said "much else that was deeply sincere" and that she spoke with "a cultivated accent and vocabulary."

Not until her second European visit did Berenson see the Dunham Dance Company perform, in October, 1952. Then he wrote, "It wakes up and brings to life in one even like myself the sleeping dogs of almost prehuman dreads, aversions, aberrations, appeals . . . How all this would have horrified most of us fifty years ago. . . . We feel at last free to return to the primitive, the infantile, the barbarous, the savage in us even the way the Greeks of the best period did in Bacchic rites, so wild, so cruel, so filthy!"

Berenson and Katherine had their first quarrel when Katherine paid a Christmas visit to I Tatti and sought Berenson's opinion about performing a ballet on lynching for her Paris audience. Choreographed in South America, this ballet had been specially requested by French leftist journalists who liked to embarrass the United States about its color prejudice. When Katherine asked the American Embassy how they felt about it, the ambassador shrugged his shoulders and said he wouldn't presume to dictate what she should put in her show. Berenson's strong opinion was that it would not be fair to her native land to show it to the rest of the world at its worst. Katherine argued the matter with him and ended by leaving I Tatti in a huff.

When the ballet was finally danced, nobody was pleased. French leftist journalists thought the lynching theme should have been presented more harshly. Journalists on the right criticized her for putting on the ballet at all. But Berenson, at least, applauded Katherine's action in a letter that apologized for trying to tell her what to do. He said that of course as an artist she had the right to present any theme about which she felt strongly enough. No subject should be forbidden.

By such disagreements and their resolutions, friendships are often deepened. Katherine and Berenson came to know one another better in many discussions they had while strolling through the jasmine-scented gardens and cypress avenues on the I Tatti estate which Berenson seldom left. When Katherine was off with her touring company in France, Denmark, or other parts of Europe, she and Berenson continued their conversations by letter.

She was having her usual ambivalent feelings about the Dunham Dance Company and their touring life.

Berenson did not see why Katherine should hang such an albatross around her neck. He thought it was folly, surely, to keep trying to support forty to fifty people when she could break away and establish a career on her own as a writer. He remarked that Katherine's work had already been published. Why not build on that and develop her writing further. Berenson called attention to the fact that Katherine had led an extraordinarily varied and interesting life and met many of the great people of the world. If she were seeking subject matter to write about, that might make a good start.

But her own life was a subject Katherine found herself unaccountably shying away from. Erich Fromm had long ago observed this tendency and once asked, "Why so much curiosity about others [in her anthropological work] and so little about yourself?" He'd also sent her biographies to read, saying that an understanding of the lives of others might be a door through which she would walk into a better understanding of her own motivations, problems, and interactions with others.

Katherine, however, was not yet ready to give up the Dunham Dance Company. Besides her love of dancing there was the special responsibility she felt as symbolic flag-bearer for the cultural march of the black race. So the Dunham troupe wove its way up and down through the countries of Europe and Scandinavia and back again on return engagements. And the troubles and perplexities continued as Katherine wondered how long she could continue to take the stresses and strains of a touring company.

In 1952, at the age of forty-three, she had to face the fact that every dancer's life is limited by the sheer physical act of growing older. Her arthritis had been giving her trouble for a long time and she could not expect it to improve with age. She thought about what had happened to other dancers. Pavlova and Isadora Duncan had danced to the time of their deaths but they had died fairly young. Martha Graham, then in her mid-fifties, was still dancing vigorously but that was exceptional. Ruth St. Denis, then seventy years old, remained active, but as a teacher rather than a performer.

Sometimes it seemed to Katherine that the Dunham school in New York might be the best answer to her questions about the future—if ever she could settle down long enough to pay some attention to it. A letter she wrote on June 24, 1952 to Doris Duke, who had once invested money in the Dunham school, tells Katherine's feelings at this time. "I so often think about what you said about teaching and have found a great pleasure teaching again during the past few weeks. There are periods when it seems especially non-productive and at other times all of the answers seem to be there in profusion. This is one of the things which has often made me wonder whether I should abandon everything else for a teaching career."

Such considerations had to be pushed to the back of

her mind while she wrestled with the accumulation of everyday details. There were contracts to be signed with performers and students; booking and travel arrangements to be organized; endless dealings with agents, lawyers, and banks. Old debts had to be paid and fresh loans arranged. Promotion and publicity had to be planned. There were tax troubles and even union problems to solve. The Dunham dance school was having its chronic financial crisis and mortgage troubles.

In late 1953, while Katherine was in Rome, she received an unhappy letter regarding the school. Dale Wasserman, a film script writer and former member of the company, was a man whose judgment Katherine respected. He wrote, "From all I can see of the [Dunham] school and its various problems I think it should be closed. It strikes me that it is costing you somewhere around $800 weekly, money which would be far more useful in clearing obligations and establishing a healthier atmosphere . . . I see no way to justify it as it stands . . . It may be you would wish to reconstitute it sometime and it may be done more meaningfully then . . ."

Unable to bear the idea of the school ending, Katherine argued for awhile that the physical premises of the school were needed as a New York base and rehearsal space for her company. Eventually she had to give in. After ten years of existence the Dunham school closed its doors in 1954. Katherine confessed, "I feel heartsick."

She then turned her attention to Habitation Leclerc to see if she could turn it into an income-producing property by putting up a small tourist hotel. But she lacked the necessary funds, and her appeals to various people to advance her the money were not successful at this time. In any event, she always meant to keep one building and Pauline's Pool for the use of herself and her family.

And by now Katherine had a family other than her dance company to consider. Perhaps to win some of the satisfactions other people enjoy in a more settled life, Katherine and John adopted a little girl in December, 1952. She was a lovely five-year-old French Martinique child of mixed parentage named Marie Christine Columbier. For awhile she went along with her new parents on their travels, before being sent to school in Switzerland.

During the fifties there were other, more direct physical problems for Katherine to deal with. She wrote Dale Wasserman, "Although I have had a most successful operation on both knees, removing lots of cartilege, and my general health is 100% better than ever I still badly want to get out of this rat-race even though I suppose it will be into another one."

As a welcome change of pace, the Dunham company became involved in the making of two films; *Mambo* in Italy, and *Cakewalk* in Mexico. Katherine also visited Africa as the palace guest of the Crown Prince of Morocco, Moulay Hassen. Watching his Royal Dancers, it occurred to her they might be used in a future Dunham show.

When Katherine and her company performed in New York for the first time in five years, in 1955, critic Walter Terry noticed Katherine's physical limitations. He said, "Miss Dunham continues to exert her quite irresistible charm without exerting herself muscularly. Indeed she rarely indulged in anything more than a hip-swaying shuffle, a mild kick or two, perhaps a backbend and facile undulations of the body. But with Miss Dunham all this is sufficient, for like Markova she can . . . make you forget that anyone else is on stage . . ."

Perhaps this mention of her limitations prompted Katherine to recall Berenson's advice, for soon after, she lunched with literary agent Margot Johnson and asked tentatively if there would be any interest in a story of her life. A women's magazine offered a fairly good sum for a short extract. Of course, the agent pointed out, a book-length biography would mean more money—but that might take a year or more to write. Katherine said she would see when she could find time to begin writing.

The Dunham Dance Company did not return to Europe the following year. Instead, bookings materialized in a part of the world the Dunham company had never visited before—Australia, New Zealand, and the Far East. This tour proved to be a disaster and a turning point.

The trip started on a rather sour note. While Katherine was struggling to support her company with monies earned from their own performances, she found it galling to read in the March 6, 1956 issue of

The New York Times that the New York City Ballet was being subsidized by the American National Theatre and Academy to make an almost identical tour. Not for the first time, Katherine resentfully wondered why she could not win such government help to support her own troupe.

"How many other Americans [as her own traveling company] are given such an opportunity to sell America?" she asked. "Even some of the more educated Europeans are astounded to find that there is educational opportunity in America for the Negro. I'd like to offset some of that false propaganda." She felt they had a unique chance to create good will and understanding abroad with United States sponsorship. But no government help was forthcoming.

Brooding over what she considered the injustice of this, fretting about the difficulties of keeping her group going, Katherine spent sleepless nights in hotel and dressing rooms as the company started its tour. She was also restlessly torn between conflicting ambitions and desires, feeling a mutual interdependence with the members of the company yet longing to be free of them. Her temper became highly unpredictable, her attitude sometimes caustic.

In Australia Katherine received a "bad press" for the first time in her life. A writer for the *Saturday Magazine* reported of a rehearsal, "I heard the Voice long before I could make out the woman in the blackness of the Tivoli Theatre . . . It was a voice which, its every inflection proclaimed, was accustomed to being obeyed . . ." He then told how he saw "A slim pale-faced youth . . . proceed to write down the words that fell from the Dunham lips as though they were Holy Writ. Miss Dunham caused gaps in the youth's stenography by sending him on errands; she had him tripping backstage, down to the orchestra pit, and all about."

Another writer for the *People News Magazine* observed, "No one addresses Katherine Dunham as anything but Miss Dunham . . . not even her husband. His wife, in return, formally addresses him as Mr. P." He noted with interest that Miss Dunham had her dressing room specially furnished for her and that "Miss Dunham . . . often sleeps there at night."

If displays of artistic temperament disgusted some, it fascinated others. One woman journalist chuckled at the fact that Katherine made people take their shoes off before entering her dressing room which she had decorated in Japanese style. The reporter was further amused at the way Katherine caused John Pratt to have a fit of nervous anxiety by flagrantly breaking her diet, dragging her mink coat around as if it were an old rag, and keeping a taxi waiting until there were only fifteen minutes left to drive ten miles to catch a plane. The journalist concluded admiringly, "She's a law unto herself."

In New Zealand a reporter tried for more depth of understanding about the complex Dunham character. Noting that Katherine had pledged a diamond necklace of her own to finance the company's Pacific tour, he said, "therein lies a clue to . . . Katherine Dunham. She sees herself as an instrument charged with one purpose: maintaining and perfecting her conception of the dance as an art form. Money, security, family —all these have been sacrificed as occasion demanded. Hard on herself, she is hard on others but despite long hours, stormy scenes and low pay—the average Dunham dancer gets only the wage of a New Zealand laborer—the company stays with her."

John Pratt did not. He ducked out for Haiti sometime before the company left the Australia-New Zealand area bound for the Orient. For the moment he had had enough. Before long he was joined by his adopted daughter who was first sent by her mother to Annette Dunham's home in Joliet, then stayed for a time with John's brother's family in Chicago before John arranged schooling for her in Haiti.

As Katherine's husband and as production supervisor to the Dunham company, John Pratt was soon sorely missed. Katherine also worried about her daughter and wrote many letters to American friends inquiring about the absent members of her family. She fretted at receiving no word from them and for a while was not even sure where they were.

As the Dunham company moved into the hot countries of Singapore and Hong Kong, tensions increased. There were troubles arranging for water coolers and fans. Katherine's devoted, long-time secretary, a Scotch-English woman named Margaret Scott, on one occasion apparently resorted to communicating with her boss through a note written by the assistant stage manager. He said that Miss Scott objected to being shouted at by Miss Dunham when she tried to explain something, and then being bawled out later for not having done so.

From Hong Kong they traveled to Manila and finally to Japan, where the sad word reached Katherine that her stepmother was desperately ill and not expected to live. Katherine's real mother and father, and her brother Albert, were already gone. After Annette Poindexter Dunham died, Katherine would be the last living member of the family she remembered from her childhood.

It may have been this sober realization, coupled with her nervous exhaustion, that finally pushed her into action. Though Katherine had repeatedly warned her dancers about her desire to quit the whole show, they never believed her. She had often made the same threats on other tours. But on October 4, 1957 the unthinkable happened and she disbanded the Dunham Dance Company.

It was not meant to be a final end to the company. She simply said she needed to free herself "for a few months in order to get some long overdue writing done." Indeed, as she became more sure about this break and the reasons for it, she was able to be more relaxed, and better relations were restored within the company. She went to a lot of trouble to try to find other jobs for them. Mutual feelings of esteem and affection were expressed. The terrible prospect of actually being without one another, after the company had been together so long, affected everyone, including Katherine.

Relations with John Pratt were also restored as Katherine received a letter from him in Haiti and then cabled her husband about Annette's illness. He answered immediately, "Sorry. Will go at once. All my love, John." Since Katherine could not break away from the final commitments of the tour, John would go to see Annette in her place, to give what comfort he could and handle the necessary arrangements.

On October 18, 1957, Annette Poindexter Dunham died peacefully in Joliet, Illinois. Soon Katherine received letters from neighbors and friends saying what a good person Annette had been and how "frequently she spoke of you with justifiable pride and adored you."

Swallowing her grief, Katherine now felt free to tell what she remembered of the childhood that had made her into the woman she had become.

IV   Some Endings and New Beginnings

13

Interlude in Japan

*A*s if resuming an interrupted conversation, Katherine wrote to literary agent Margot Johnson in New York on November 21, 1957. "You honestly should be one to know what is going on in my life at this moment, especially since you are to some degree responsible. Finally I've done what I've threatened to do over the years but no one believed it, least of all I. Here in Tokyo . . . we finished our Australia Orient tour and it seemed a good time to send the company onward for a much promised separation. It all sounds so simple but has been and is very complicated and makes for much anguish and separation blues and future-uncertainty on all sides. A good thing seems to be a tenacious decision on my part to write . . ."

To her friend, Doris Duke, Katherine wrote in more detail. "I am pleased that the termination of one cycle of my career should have occurred in a locale at least interesting . . . It is just 20 years since the founding of the company and I have just closed it for its first voluntary leave. Suddenly . . . the struggle and responsibility and anguish and strife seemed an utter absurdity and I knew that the only way to save the battered remnants of a self that I never actually even knew was to stop and give it a chance. So I warned [the company] for some months and then just quit. John has been in Haiti for a year now and his absence added to the burdens of the company . . . Now I am trying to swing into a rhythm of writing . . . I am starting [the book] with my first meeting with Berenson in Florence."

Katherine credited Berenson for having persuaded her to take up a writing career. She said he was "wonderful, writing constant encouragement," always assuring her that she could have "a more gratifying creative life and even more financial security by writing than in the theatre."

Looking around for a suitable place to settle down and work, Katherine found an attic that had formerly been a tailor's shop. Its windows gave Katherine a view of Mount Fuji seen through pine trees over the wooden roofs of Tokyo "just like in the prints in art stores" she told friends. From the company's props came matting, curtains, a double bench, and gold chairs to help furnish the large, bare room. Katherine added her own hi-fi set and a handsome black lacquer Chinese chest that she borrowed. She also had a table and chair to set out on the rooftop terrace where she could work in good weather.

At first Katherine thought the book she wanted to write would be about members of the Dunham Company and their touring experiences. She planned to have dancer Lucille Ellis, the member of the company who had been with her longest, stay awhile to help her reminisce. Katherine even chose a title for the book. It was to be called *The Insatiables* because so ofen she couldn't figure out exactly what it was that her troupe wanted of her, or of their own lives. Though Katherine had done the best she could for them, she was aware that her dancers felt continually restless and discontent.

Katherine thought there might be other parts of her life that would be more interesting to write about. She wasn't sure. She spoke of her uncertainty to Margot Johnson. "To date it has been a gathering together of notes and transferring them to bits of paper to more permanent form; and a battle in semi-darkness to find what is the right thing to write now . . . I have a struggle not to begin with childhood and unravel a lot that has been brought closer to the surface by my mother's death."

She confessed, "One of my grave problems is financial, Margot . . ." Among her debts was money owed on projects being done at Habitation Leclerc. With her encouragement, John Pratt was restoring the house and going ahead with other plans and improvements to make the place attractive to tourists. Dale Wasserman, staying in Haiti with John for a time, reported to Katherine that about $14,000 was needed to complete the work already under way.

Katherine's young adopted daughter, Marie Christine, was receiving local schooling in Haiti. A motherly woman who ran a *pension* was helping John Pratt take care of her. There was no point in having the child come to Japan, where Katherine could not look after her properly. The best contribution she could make to the family was to continue work on her book.

Spurred by necessity, Katherine urged Margot to try to get a lump sum down payment from the women's magazine that had formerly expressed interest in her life story. She typed out a list of other magazines and suggested that Margot try to get additional bids from them.

Patiently the literary agent explained that as yet Katherine had produced only scraps of experience that needed to be pulled together before they would be saleable. Further, if Katherine had a book in mind, the book must be sold prior to parcelling out sections to magazines. Otherwise the book would be weakened and its publication imperilled.

Katherine was convinced that what she was writing was a book and also that she wanted the book to be a best seller. She could think of nothing else to dig herself out of the financial hole she was in. If a theatrical agent could offer her $25,000 for a twelve week personal tour, Katherine felt publishers should be able to match that bid.

A letter came from a top editor of the publishing company currently considering Katherine's unfinished manuscript. He said that the outlines submitted by Katherine so far would not turn out the best seller she wanted. If Katherine would come to New York to have a conference with them he believed "we could tailor-make a book that would please the majority of magazine readers as well as the book buyers." To win such an audience, however, the editor said Katherine must emphasize the more glamorous episodes in her career and lace her story with frequent mention of the celebrities she had known. He said Katherine should recognize the fact that writing is far different from dancing which is carried along by music, color, and action.

Hurt by the raw frankness with which the editor spoke, Katherine was thrown back on herself sufficiently to get better acquainted with her own feelings. To her great credit she defended their sincerity and depth. In her letter of reply to the editor Katherine said: "I am convinced that our two ideas of autobiography differ and, more serious, that what I must say of myself at this time is not what I am expected to say of myself, particularly by those who do not know me very well . . . I had hoped that the book would rest on its own literary merit rather than on those facts of my life which might arouse and satisfy certain curiosities of people who have thought only of the person who has wandered through forty-seven countries and God knows how many stages in the past years. This same person had to be made up of some kind of earth as well as star material, and the book that I am now deeply immersed in, with more love and care than I imagined I would be capable of devoting to anything [will examine] the composition of the person who grew into the institution, which is my favorite and somewhat deprecatory way of referring to the self that runs the Dunham Company. I have tender feelings for the girl and for the family and feel that at this stage of my life they must both be explained."

Katherine went on to say that "the Aly Kahns and Dukes and Rubirosas can wait . . . I thought I had made it clear that all of this is in the second book, *The Insatiables* . . . I have to be made and presented before my deeds take importance."

In the three or four volume autobiography of her life that Katherine now projected, it was her childhood she wanted to write about first. "I find a burning desire to know more about the girl," she said of herself as a child.

Such lack of empathy between the writer and the book editor caused agent Margot Johnson to take Katherine's manuscript to another publisher. While it rested there Katherine continued feverishly recording more episodes from her childhood. By May she had written over 150,000 words and the devoted Miss

Scott had typed the pages cleanly to send off, a section at a time, to her agent in New York. Copies were also sent to Bernard Berenson who faithfully read them and sent back helpful comments.

Between chapters, Katherine let loose another, louder public blast at the United States government for their failure to sponsor her company on tours abroad. She accused the American National Theatre and Academy of neglecting black artists.

A prompt reply came from ANTA stating that over ten percent of the performers they had assisted were blacks such as Leontyne Price, the Dizzy Gillespie jazz band, Marian Anderson, and others. They said their limited funds permitted them to aid only those people or companies unable to make foreign tours on their own. They politely pointed out that no formal application from the Dunham Dance Company had ever been received. If she cared to submit one it would go before a distinguished dance panel made up of professionals undoubtedly already well known to her, such as dance critic Walter Terry, choreographer Agnes de Mille, and Doris Humphrey, who would certainly consider Katherine's application "with the greatest sympathy and sincerity."

Katherine may have felt that an application would take too long to process, or would be a "one time only" kind of assistance. For whatever reason she did not pursue the matter further. Instead, in late May she contracted for the usual booking agent's arrangements for the Dunham Dance Company to tour again in Europe. However, Katherine assured her literary agent, this tour would not start until she had completed the writing she had started.

In June the second publisher to consider Katherine's manuscript turned her down. Margot Johnson took the manuscript to a third publisher who had asked to see it. This was Harcourt Brace who, like the other publishers, thought a personal conference with the author would be desirable.

Katherine avoided such invitations to New York because she feared the Internal Revenue Service might pounce on her for unpaid back taxes. Yet if she didn't get a book advance from the publishers, how was she to raise the cash to pay her taxes or anything else? It was a vicious circle broken by an offer of film work in Hollywood. Katherine was asked to choreograph and direct the dance sequences for *Green Mansions*, a movie based on W. H. Hudson's tale of idyllic life in the forest. Katherine was assured that if she made some accommodations with the Internal Revenue Service prior to taking the job there would be no trouble. Such an arrangement was worked out, freeing Katherine to return to the United States.

She was working in Hollywood when she received the good news that Harcourt Brace was seriously interested in publishing her book but thought a lot of rewriting had to be done. Katherine agreed to this and won a book contract. Unable to write in the Hollywood atmosphere, she decided to rejoin her family in Haiti.

At Habitation Leclerc she worked hard and well.

Shortly before Christmas, 1958, the last chapter of *A Touch Of Innocence*, described by Katherine as "the story of the first painful eighteen years of my life," was finished. Feeling relieved and purged at having finished the book, Katherine threw herself into another kind of activity until it would be published. She opened a medical clinic. This came about almost by accident, and started with a tragically ironic story.

One day Katherine came across her caretaker and a few workmen rolling on the ground, doubled up with mirth, and she asked to be let in on the joke. Gasping for breath between fits of laughter they told Katherine a true incident that had just happened. A poor young peasant couple, having a sick baby, walked five miles to the city clinic and were told the infant needed an expensive medicine which must be injected immediately to save its life. Not having enough money to buy this medicine, they walked five miles back to their village to beg, borrow, and pawn all they had to raise the required sum of about two dollars. Taking the money they walked another five miles back to the city to get the prescription filled at the pharmacy, and then walked to the clinic where they had to wait an hour for the doctor to be free.

Coming to see them at last, the doctor discovered that the baby, held all this time in a blanket in its mother's arms, had died sometime during these journeys. The doctor, reasoning that the couple no longer had any use for the medicine they'd bought, took it from them and put it in his own pocket.

Katherine understood that laughter was the workmen's way of dealing with an impossible situation. But she was appalled at the story. She wondered why it had not occurred to her before that medical aid for the poor was one of the greatest needs in Haiti. That afternoon she sent off a letter to her New York physician, describing the situation and asking for his help.

Shortly she received "a mammoth supply of sample remedies for internal parasites of many kinds, for malaria, influenza, tuberculosis, yaws and other ailments." Included were instructions for using these medicines. With the temporary help of two local doctors Katherine proceeded to work "miracle cures" on hundreds of outpatients and about a half dozen inpatients monthly.

Working a twelve hour day starting at seven A.M. she reported that energies "formerly used on stage or at typewriter went into therapeutic massage, injections, cleansing and salving ulcers, boiling needles, worming babies, and other clinic demands . . . President Duvalier on his visit did not seem greatly impressed . . ."

This was disappointing since Haitian President François Duvalier, known as Papa Doc, was a true medical doctor who had graduated from Cornell University in the United States. Perhaps, Katherine reasoned, he thought her clinic facilities, with outdoor cooking pots utilized to boil water, were too crude.

Or there might be other reasons. Friends whispered to Katherine that Papa Doc might disapprove of the clinic activities as tending to undercut the usual de-

pendence of the population on Voodoo doctors. Voodoo, they said, was one of Papa Doc's means of keeping the people under his thumb.

François Duvalier had emerged as a strong man
from a period of chaos that followed Paul Magloire's
unsuccessful attempt to stay on as President after his
term was over. Magloire was now in exile, like Dumarsais Estimé.

According to political rumors, Magloire had long
been feathering his nest with dollar bills held in bank
accounts outside Haiti. The cynics said he had enough
to lead a long, rich life. But Estimé, dead in 1953 of a
"broken heart for home and country" was still revered by the Haitian people. This included Duvalier
who greatly respected him and spoke to Katherine
bitterly of how Estimé had been betrayed by the
army.

Because of Duvalier's admiration for such a man as
Estimé, Katherine did not share the deep apprehension other Haitians felt about Duvalier's rise to power.
Duvalier's appearance alone was enough to frighten
many people. With full lips down-turned, eyes hidden behind thick, dark glasses, and a complexion of a
grayish hue, Duvalier bore a strong resemblance to
Baron Samedi, one of the feared gods of cemeteries
and death.

Many Haitians soon discovered that this menacing
appearance was more than just a façade. Distrust of
the regular army had led Duvalier to create his own
militia from the ranks of the proleteriat. They devel-

oped into a band of ruthless hoodlums earning the name of Ton-ton Macoute, meaning Uncle with the Big Stick. These sticks—and guns—were used to terrorize peasants into submission, and businessmen into bankruptcy. Besides ousting the rich from their homes and plantations, the Ton-ton Macoute frightened away tourists and diverted foreign aid into their own pockets.

But this intimidation and pillage was gradual at the onset, and not very evident in early 1958. At any rate, it did not seem to threaten Habitation Leclerc or its inhabitants, unless running a clinic might bring down their wrath.

To help counteract any offense she might have given Duvalier, Katherine offered him a portion of her own land for the Haitian people to use as a botanical garden and bird sanctuary, and a natural open air theatre. In a special audience that Duvalier granted her, Katherine spoke persuasively about the benefits that could result from encouraging tourist trade and winning United States financial help.

Graciously, Duvalier said he thought it was time she got promoted from Chevalier in the Haitian Legion of Honor to become a Commander and Grand Officer. This badge of office was a heavy cross on a broad ribbon that was hung around her neck in February, 1959, by the Haitian Minister of Foreign Affairs, a personal friend. Another good friend, the mayor of Port-au-Prince, named Katherine an honorary citizen of Haiti. Newspaper accounts said "Miss

Dunham responded with words of gratitude, express-
ing her long established feeling of being a daughter of
Haiti."

She meant it sincerely. Haiti and a thriving tourist
business at Habitation Leclerc were now her hope for
future security. Politically she must watch her step
and be as diplomatic as possible. As far as the clinic
was concerned, Katherine was ready to close it down
since she had to leave for the Dunham Dance Company's upcoming third European tour.

Then it was suggested that someone else take over
the clinic during her absence. Katherine was told
about a man who was the "perfect choice," someone
who had funds to start a feeding station for mothers
and babies and who might even introduce "the
delicate subject of birth control." Though Katherine
had long yearned to start both these activities herself,
she refused the offer.

This was a more astute political decision than she
knew. After the man who had been proposed as clinic
head had left Haiti, Katherine learned that he had
planned to use the clinic as a cover-up to conceal arms
and ammunition that would be used to try to over-
throw the Duvalier regime. She had no wish to risk
being in the middle of a revolution.

Christmas cards sent to Katherine for the 1959 holi-
day season bore congratulations from friends and relatives on her book, *A Touch Of Innocence*, which was
at last published and favorably reviewed. A *New York
Times* critic called it "one of the most extraordinary

life stories I have ever read . . . Not one breath of sentimentality or self-pity mars or falsifies the clear picture of her girlhood, her family and her surroundings . . . The anthropological method she learned has been absorbed and assimilated into a way of looking at the world with a kind of exact, tolerant, but not uncritical justice. The proper word for it, I think, is wisdom. This story of a childhood and youth becomes a mature exploration of the human spirit, its perils and its dignities . . ."

The dedication page in front of the book bore the inscription, "To B.B." Katherine had not forgotten the inspiration of Bernard Berenson who died, age 94, the same year the book came out.

14

Snakes in Paradise

On the Dunham Dance Company's third European tour—which added Greece, Lebanon, and Austria to the countries they had visited before—there were the usual temperamental, emotional, and financial troubles. Again there came a point when strange foods and languages and accommodations seemed more bothersome than exciting. Quarrels were magnified in the confines of a small group. Sometimes they couldn't get the right theatre, or any theatre, for their performances. And there was the endless worry of having to support forty people during long waits between bookings, with no money coming in.

These difficulties exploded with volcanic force in

Vienna and the Dunham company fell apart. But along the way they had met a young man who wanted to take part in what seemed to him to be their glamorous existence. The son of comfortably fixed Scandinavian parents, he was twenty-four years old with no particular goal in life. At the age of fifty-one, Katherine Dunham was feeling, as she said in a letter, "jaded morally and physically with little hope of encountering someone who had real humanity and wonder and love and creative sensibility."

To this lost youth, she attributed all those qualities. She blamed Dick Frisell's undisciplined ways on lack of purpose, and she believed that his life would be more constructive if he found work he enjoyed doing.

There was plenty of work to be done at Habitation Leclerc. From Spain, where Katherine stayed awhile, she left for Haiti and Dick Frisell went with her. Since he had a great interest in animals, Katherine encouraged him to start a small zoo on the grounds as a tourist attraction. He also invested money to help finance some buildings on the property.

From New York, John Pratt helped expedite the shipment of various small animals for the new zoo before he returned to Haiti. Meanwhile Katherine was busy supervising the construction of five bungalow hotel units, the Bar Geisha decorated in Japanese style, and the Salon Guinée nightclub with its African motif.

By 1961 Habitation Leclerc was seriously advertising for tourist business. Its facilities were pictured over French and German TV, described to American readers in a United Press story and in an article in *The New York Times* Sunday Travel Section. A brochure was put out describing the attractions and the grounds.

Among the entertainments offered by Habitation Leclerc were afternoon tea dances, a zoological exhibit, lunch or dinner with "excellent cuisine under the personal supervision of Miss Dunham," Voodoo ceremonial dancing, a tropical forest to walk through, a "romantic evening beside Pauline's swimming pool" where visitors would be serenaded by a strolling minstrel, as well as a nightclub show and ballroom dancing to a live orchestra.

It was a gallant bid for business and a lot of hard work went into it. Inevitably it aroused jealousy among some people, leading to troubles "of a type that can be found only in Haiti" as Katherine later told the story to a United States newspaper.

Besides his small animals and birds of bright plumage, young Dick had imported some Amazon and African pythons. Somehow a couple of these escaped, and it was rumored they were highly dangerous. Through frequent announcements over the local radio, and by word of mouth, the rumors spread and grew. It was said that one snake had swallowed several children on their way to school. Another story was that a woman and her donkey had disappeared down a snake's throat as they were riding to town. Letters to the editor bombarded the local newspaper, spreading alarm. Soon the snakes would overrun the island, they said, eating everyone and everything in sight. This constituted a threat to the government.

In the terror-saturated reign of Duvalier, the possibility of swift official punishment for some fancied offense was always present. Katherine was particularly sensitive to this, having been unable to arrange another interview with Duvalier since her last return from Europe. She did not know why she was being rebuffed. Perhaps Duvalier was disappointed that hopes for American aid had not been realized. Perhaps he feared tourism might introduce new ideas, or invite a comparison of living standards that could weaken his hold on the people.

But it was impossible to know what Duvalier thought, or might do. Once several of his Ton-ton Macoute came to the threshold of Habitation Leclerc. The masons hid behind their stones, the carpenters were lost in a barrage of hammering—every worker or guard on the estate suddenly found urgent business elsewhere, or looked in another direction. So Katherine angrily drove off the ruffians herself.

She knew the danger of such defiance. It was a time when, to avoid torture, jail, or assassination, countless Haitians were fleeing the island even though it meant abandoning everything, including family. Hotels, villas, and other businesses were torn apart and plundered to furnish luxuries to the ever-greedy Ton-ton Macoute. Why, then, had she succeeded in making them spare Leclerc?

Katherine could attribute it only to a basic friend-liness Duvalier must feel for her despite his stony silence. This indirect friendliness was again demon-strated during the snake scare when Duvalier ordered all the zoo's snakes banished to the government farm instead of sending his strong men back to Leclerc.

But tourism does not flourish in this kind of atmo-sphere. There were few boats dropping anchor at Haiti, and few tourists getting off to stay even for a day on the island. Those who ventured ashore were soon disheartened by pursuing bands of crippled beg-gars, streets with open sewage drains, and the sight of festering slums. The Ton-ton Macoute, in the guise of taxi drivers, insisted on trying to "play guide, pro-curer, gigolo, escort and business manager to the help-less tourist" as Katherine later described it. The tour-ists fled back to their boats as quickly as they could get there.

Until conditions changed Katherine had to find another way to make a living. She started a local dance school which again stirred up so much jealousy from a school already established in Port-au-Prince that she had to abandon the project. She went after the job of choreographing a New York show but lost out to choreographer Agnes de Mille, a friend of hers. She discussed business details with Eartha Kitt about do-ing the dance sequences for a musical play in which her former student might be starred. Katherine also considered working up a small act of her own with Dunham Dance Company members Lenwood Morris and Vanoye Aikens—an act that might travel to Miami and the western nightclub circuit.

Lenwood Morris was already in Haiti, heading the dance school, but Vanoye Aikens was working in a film in Rome. Katherine sent him an airmail letter proposing the small act idea. In his answer, Aikens allowed himself the rare privilege of being openly, wittily impudent to his former boss.

Replying July 12, 1961, Aikens let Katherine know he still was unhappy about the breakup of the company in Vienna. Before he could consider Katherine's present offer he must tell her that he had medical bills in Rome that had to be paid, that he'd expect to receive transportation costs, that he must postpone or break off other film commitments at some loss to himself, and that he now commanded a salary of five hundred a week. As he listed his terms, one by one, Aikens headed each with the mischievous remark, "Worser and Worser." Summing it all up he concluded that Katherine should probably get herself another dancing partner. Then he boldly gave some advice: "I know you like to write and all that but you belong in action on a stage. So buy some metrecal or whatever that new fangled reducing mixture is called and get with it."

Like everyone else associated with Katherine, Aikens knew her love of good food and tendency to put on weight—particularly now when she was heading a tourist restaurant. Katherine's cordial answer to this letter showed rare controlled good humor. She said that if her contract with Eartha Kitt came through she would keep his demands in mind and get the best terms possible. Meanwhile it was nice to know that Aikens was being kept so busy with movie work. She ended wistfully by asking, "How about agenting me for a film?"

That summer of 1961 she finished an outline for the next section of her life story and sent it to Harcourt Brace. She had her usual troubles with organization. Her "amorphous style," as one publisher called it, wove back and forth confusingly in time. Harcourt editor Dan Wickenden stated his confidence that she would shape up the material eventually. But, for the moment there was no contract and no advance on the book.

The business that finally harnessed her energies was not one she had sought. Stephen Papich, a successful Hollywood producer who had been a student at the Dunham dance school in New York, thought the time was ripe for Katherine to do another big, touring revue. Katherine proposed that the show's theme be based on Africa. Papich liked that idea.

Since 1953, when she had been a palace guest of the Crown Prince, Katherine had remembered the extraordinary dancers from many villages of Morocco who had performed before her at the Prince's request. Now she thought it would be a great coup if such dancers could be featured in the new show. Following lengthy negotiations, the former Crown Prince of Morocco, now King Hassen II, gave his consent.

But that was only the beginning. During May and June of 1962 Katherine Dunham, Stephen Papich, John Pratt, and Dick Frisell traveled thousands of miles through western Africa looking for talent. They auditioned dancers, musicians, and singers in Morocco, Senegal, Nigeria, and Guinea, choosing twenty-five performers to bring back with them for the show.

They also captured a few old-time Dunham Dance Company members along the way, such as the humorously irreverent Vanoye Aikens, Ural Wilson, Lenwood Morris—and Lucille Ellis who joked that she was probably "the only American female dancer who did not appear in *Cleopatra*," the movie which Aikens and Wilson had both been working on in Rome. Settings and costumes for the new Dunham revue were to be done by John Pratt. A lot of the old gang was back together again.

Opening October 22, 1962 at the 54th Street Theatre in New York, *Bamboche* was divided into three acts. The first introduced the dancers from Morocco; the second was a dance-drama set in South Africa called "The Diamond Thief"; and the third act featured American gospel singing and jazz.

Most critics thought "The Diamond Thief," choreographed by Katherine Dunham, was the best part of the show. The whole was "wonderfully rowdy . . . gorgeously staged . . . unabashedly theatrical" but the reviewers agreed that it also "has something to say about folklore and change . . . You could even say that Miss Dunham, who actually did start out her career as an anthropologist, is still something of a teacher as she discloses through her dances the irritations, temptations, lusts and beauties, traditions and anachronisms in the changing world of the modern African."

But many avid theater goers had their minds on something else that summer. Intermediate range missiles had been installed in Cuba by the Soviet Union with the encouragement of Cuban Premier Fidel Castro. Harsh words were being exchanged between Russia and the United States as President John Kennedy protested that these missiles posed a threat to Americans. Until the Russians agreed to pull them out the country was on edge.

Then came a newspaper strike that led to a long blackout of all seven major New York newspapers from December, 1962 to mid-March, 1963. Unable to use advertising to overcome the sluggish response of their potential audience, producer Stephen Papich gave up and closed *Bamboche*.

That left members of the Dunham Dance Company stranded but at least in New York where they could look for other work. Katherine, who was staying at the Chelsea Hotel, decided to hire extra space and start another dance school.

The Chelsea's hospitality to artists, writers, poets, and musicians was legendary. In the course of its history it had sheltered such writers and poets as O. Henry, Thomas Wolfe, Mark Twain, Edgar Lee Masters, the painter John Sloane, the actress Anna

Russell, the playwright Arthur Miller, and many others. With a reputation for running "the world's most tolerant hotel" the Chelsea management did not object to exotic pets or plants or odd behavior.

But now the steady playing of the Dunham School's African bongo drums caused an insurrection that split the hotel right down the middle. Sides were formed among the tenants and petitions signed to actually throw a guest out of the Chelsea "for insufferable disturbance." The manager, on the verge of tears at such a happening, was quoted as saying, "I'm just a crazy Hungarian. I like people."

A compromise was reached where it was agreed that Katherine Dunham could continue living at the hotel but the drums had to go. Katherine moved her school to rented quarters at 440 West 42nd Street.

In an interview at that time, Katherine gave her reasons for reviving the school. She was tired of wandering, for the time being, she said. She felt that she needed "to stop and do some thinking and develop somewhat more. Another thing, I feel I should defend the school and technique I pioneered in. I should clarify it more and protect and develop it."

The Dunham technique was used in an opera for the first time in 1963 when Katherine was asked to choreograph and stage the dances for *Aida* as produced at the Metropolitan Opera House for their winter season. A storm of controversy developed over the results.

Some reviewers said Katherine would "take her

place beside the lustrous Mezzo Marian Anderson and
the former prima ballerina, Janet Collins, among the
distinguished . . . artists who've appeared as Metropolitan Opera stars." However, critic Walter Terry,
usually a Dunham fan, stated flatly that the dances
might be "Dandy for Voodoo but not for Verdi."
Another paper said that though her belly dancers,
camp followers, and desert girls were "historically
and ethnically probably the most authentic ever done"
the audience was unprepared to have their attention
taken away from the music.

In her own defense, Katherine said she loved the
arias and duets in the opera but she found the dancing
music pretty dull. "If Verdi were alive today he'd
throw it out and do something new!" she claimed.

Before the end of 1963 Katherine got a chance to
speak officially to members of the United States government to tell how hard it had been to support her
own troupe for the years they had toured abroad. She
was invited to appear before a Senate subcommittee
considering whether a National Arts Council should
be founded. Katherine said that in her opinion it was
essential for American money to subsidize American
arts, and particularly American traveling companies,
to help uphold American prestige abroad.

About artists themselves, in any field, she said,
"Unfortunately I think there is a general discouragement about being able to perform with any security
and continuity. . . ."

The winning of support for her own security and

continuity was closer at hand than she knew. The disparate puzzle pieces of her life were at last being pulled together to form a cohesive picture. It began with an invitation to spend eleven weeks as artist-in-residence at Southern Illinois University in Carbondale to do the choreography and staging of the opera *Faust*.

15

Reflections in the World's Mirror

*T*he story of *Faust* was well known to Katherine. Years before she had been given the book by her old friend and adviser, Erich Fromm —at about the same time he had asked that probing question, "Why so much curiosity about others and so little about yourself?" *Faust* is a classic tale of good and evil bound to interest anyone trying to understand the nature of human beings.

The original Dr. Faustus story, based on medieval legends, was about a man who struck a bargain with the devil that his soul would go to hell when he died but in return the devil was to procure anything the man wanted during his life on earth. A restless and ambitious man, Faustus—or Faust as he came to be known in later versions of the story—wanted nothing less than to be the "great Emperor of the world."

To Katherine this strongly suggested Adolf Hitler, whose string of military successes as his Nazi troops swept over Europe had certainly verged on the diabolical. Hitler's treatment of captive peoples—the Nazi concentration camps and extermination centers for Jews—seemed like a bargain that had been struck with the devil.

So for her version of the Faust opera, Katherine chose the locale of Germany during World War II. As a newspaper reviewer described it, the curtain opened on a scene of "stark horror with bodies frozen in their action, strung on wires, on stumps of trees, and on the ground . . . Two athletes played basketball with a skeleton head . . . a child in a coffin is carried by six lightly clad females led by a Walkyrian strip-teaser and as a gigantic climax a black jacketed motor-cyclist roars across the stage . . ."

Presented February 13 and 14, 1965 on the Carbondale campus of Southern Illinois University, Katherine Dunham's *Faust* was a spectacular event. "There was seldom any doubt that the performers were amateurs but there was also constant proof that the direction was professional," concluded the review in the St. Louis Globe-Democrat. As a whole, the reporter said, it was "an exciting evening."

Katherine's residence at the university campus served to remind her of the federal and foundation help she had received as a young woman in Chicago, and she realized that the time was now ripe to win support for her efforts to help her own people.

One of the proclaimed aims of her New York dance school was "to stimulate the interest of and prepare a working program for young people of deprived backgrounds who [otherwise] have no opportunity to pursue these studies . . ."

In the 1960's there was increasing sentiment to promote such goals. Blacks were militantly demanding advantages previously denied them and many whites were championing their cause. In 1963 there was the March on Washington by two hundred thousand blacks and whites to demand better treatment for Afro-Americans. In 1964, the same year that riots erupted in Watts and Harlem, and three young white civil rights workers were murdered in Mississippi, President Lyndon Johnson pushed through the most progressive and comprehensive civil rights bill ever enacted. But passing laws about civil rights does not end inequities overnight. There was still a lot of work to be done. Katherine was invited to join a number of organizations such as the Artists' Civil Rights Assistance Fund, the Harlem Cultural Council Steering Committee, and others.

The greatest thrust of her efforts, however, went into a proposal for a pilot project in East St. Louis. It was an ambitious program based on current events and her own experiences. In the proposal she said, "East St. Louis has been the focal point of racial resentments, riots, delinquency and poverty for many years. Its situation close to the metropolis of St. Louis and still deprived of the benefits usually emanating from a metropolis because of its high Negro population, has kept the area a sensitive one."

Continuing with her thesis, she said, "The need for objectives to replace crime and delinquency, for disciplines for the leisure time of the young, the necessity in the face of increasing poverty to provide the essentials of human sustenance . . . are grave preoccupations." She proposed that her kind of dance school, which also taught such subjects as psychology, anthropology, and languages, would do this kind of neighborhood a lot of good. "The project presented reaches far beyond dance in the popular definition . . . Dance as it would serve the East St. Louis project is concerned with the fundamentals of human society."

The paper was presented to Sargent Shriver in Washington, D.C. in March, 1965. An answer to her proposal could not be expected immediately and there were still many details to be worked out. Meanwhile Katherine gave a lecture and demonstration at S.I.U. on the desirability of establishing a Department of Dance there. Assisting her was Vanoye Aikens who, when the occasion called for it, "came to my rescue . . . many times" as Katherine gladly acknowledged.

Katherine kept other members of her dance company busy whenever she could. She used them in *The Bible*, a movie which she took time off from S.I.U. to choreograph in Rome. The Dunham dancers also performed on the occasion of the 25th anniversary of the

American Ballet Theatre at the Grand Ballroom of the New York Waldorf Astoria. Undoubtedly she would use as many of her dance company as possible in any new school she might start at East St. Louis. They had the experience, and she still thought of them as her extended family.

Several other jobs came up to choreograph theatrical musical productions in Paris and Rome. Then Katherine was invited to Africa to help train the Senegalese National Ballet and serve as technical cultural adviser to Senegal's President Léopold Sédar Senghor, putting on the First World Festival of Negro Arts at Dakar, Senegal, in 1965 and 1966.

Unfortunately, disagreement over the word "negritude" almost split the festival apart. To President Senghor it meant the black races should develop an art and culture based on their own traditions—which was his inspiration for creating such a festival. Others argued that there should be "something more substantial and more universal than trying to find security in some form of esthetic black nationalism."

With her anthropological training, Katherine was more aware than most of the constant interchange and intermixing of all cultures. She had noted that "even in the farthest reaches of tribal life certain contacts with the outside world are inevitable." She said she had seen many African dances better and more purely preserved in Haiti than in the country where they had originated.

She had a story to tell. "A few years ago in Paris I

saw a documentary film made in Brazil. In what was supposed to be an authentic macumba ceremony deep in the jungle I saw movements from one of our own numbers from North Africa!" That had happened because some of the South American dancers had worked with the Dunham Company and, returning to their native villages, had taken Dunham steps with them. It was one small example of cultural exchange at work. The same thing had been true in Haiti where Katherine saw authentic Voodoo participants using steps she had introduced when, as a student, she had visited the Cul-de-Sac to join in their dances and become a Voodoo initiate.

For Katherine the word negritude became almost meaningless since she did not feel that any particular label was necessary for whatever blacks were or did. She did not believe it possible or desirable for people of any one specific color or nationality to exist alone any more.

As a student at the Sorbonne President Senghor had seen Katherine's dance company perform in Paris. The same was true of many other African chiefs. So Africa, besides being the mother of her people and the source of the dance study Katherine had been making all her life, was a place where she already had many friends. In this big, exciting country the small part most familiar to her was Senegal. Like Haiti it was a seacoast black republic formerly a piece of the vast French Colonial Empire and still deeply bound to French culture and traditions. This, too, made

Katherine feel at home—enough to consider leasing a house in Dakar, the Senegalese capital.

Her friendships with many top Senegalese leaders enabled Katherine to get a home in a neighborhood generally reserved for diplomats and government officials, near the palace of President Senghor. In 1966, Katherine and John rented a white-pillared house with a porch and balcony running its full length. That did not mean they had abandoned Haiti. Indeed Katherine took the trouble of linking the two homes symbolically by taking herbs from Habitation Leclerc to Senegal and soil from Senegal back to Habitation Leclerc.

But they were spending much less time in Haiti in the mid-1960's. One reason was Katherine's contract with Doubleday to do a book based on her life in Haiti. While recalling her experiences there, Katherine preferred to keep an objective distance, and set up her typewriter in her new Senegalese home.

The title of this book was *Island Possessed*. It was highly recommended by the critics for its remarkably frank, fascinating narrative of Katherine's complicated personal confrontations with Haiti and the Haitians over a long period of time. On the dedication page Katherine said *Island Possessed* was "a book written with love, dedicated to my husband, John Pratt, and to the Republic of Haiti explaining, I think, many things about this author and about that island."

Though outspoken about the tyranny and imperfections of Duvalier's presidency, the book was even well received by him. After reading the copy of the book that Katherine sent him, Duvalier wrote a letter thanking her "for loving my country." Further, he said "I derived extreme pleasure from reading your precious work; it conveys to the reader the true personality of the nation and the Haitian people." The letter was signed, "Dr. François Duvalier, President for Life of the Republic."

Where Estimé and Magloire had both failed to perpetuate their terms in office through parliamentary means, the one-man rule of Duvalier had succeeded in forcing his presidency-for-life down the people's throats. Similarly, President Léopold Sédar Senghor of Senegal first absorbed the office of premier into his presidency, later banished all opposition parties, and ran an unopposed list of his own candidates to victory. Then, in 1969, when workers and students went on strike against austerity measures he was forced to declare a state of emergency.

It is hard to be a new republic trying to survive in the world. It is also hard to live in one, and the plane fare to Africa is too steep to fly there from the United States on short vacations. Katherine Dunham and her husband gave up their house in Dakar in 1969. The most compelling reason for leaving was the East St. Louis project. To hold that job they would have to live as well as work in the United States.

16

Breaking Through Apathy

*I*n a lifetime full of challenges, the East St. Louis project may have been the biggest Katherine had ever faced. One problem was solved when funding was granted by several philanthropic organizations to support the work of Southern Illinois University, but a lot of other difficulties remained. How could Katherine get through to the young residents of the ghetto that she wanted to reach? How could she help to break the vicious circle of poverty, ugliness, and crime in which many ghetto youths seemed entrapped?

Generally, the idea was to open college opportunities to these young blacks so they could get better jobs and a chance to change their life style. Conventional educational techniques had failed. Katherine believed if young people were involved in something they did well and enjoyed doing—such as dancing—their confidence might be built up and they would be able to try to study other subjects.

She explained something about her aims to a Southern Illinois University student reporter: "What we are trying to do is break through apathy. It's not so much teaching people to perform as it is teaching them, through performing, that they have individual worth and can relate to other people."

Katherine's official title was Visiting Artist in the Fine Arts Division of S.I.U.'s Edwardsville campus near East St. Louis. She had not been on campus long when the first test came. With her daughter Marie Christine, now nineteen years old, and Jeanelle Stovall, a vacationing United Nations interpretor from New York, Katherine was invited to a tavern to meet a group of youths calling themselves the Imperial War Lords. The invitation came through a boy named Darryl Braddix who'd been accepted in Katherine's new East St. Louis education program. Katherine had asked Braddix to put her in touch with others who might be similarly interested, and this tavern meeting, in July 1967, was the result.

They had finished their talks and Braddix and another youth were walking the three women back to their car when the police arrested both young men. Following along to the police station Katherine insisted on knowing what the charge was and if the youths were going to get legal representation. A policeman told her to mind her own business. Katherine then walked behind the booking desk to demand information. This area was reserved for police, as the police dispatcher explained it, and he asked her to leave. When she refused, a tussle resulted in which Jeanelle Stovall tried to help Katherine and both women were jailed and charged with disorderly conduct.

Braddix had been implicated by another black youth who said he and Braddix had smashed windows in a black section of the city the night before. He was charged with criminal damage of property and held on ten thousand dollars bail. The arrest of Katherine Dunham in her efforts to see that his rights were observed made headlines. The story, featured in newspapers all over the country the next morning, aroused indignation.

Embarrassed by the publicity, authorities of East St. Louis tried to make amends, presenting Katherine Dunham with the key to the city. On one side of the key is written, "The Heart of Southwestern Illinois Metropolis—East St. Louis." On the other side is the name of Mayor Alvin G. Fields.

But the more important key, to the hearts of the people, was perhaps won that day, without fanfare or engraved words. Katherine had gone to bat for some of the people she wanted to help. After that they could more easily believe in her.

By December Katherine had become Cultural

Affairs Consultant to the Edwardsville campus of S.I.U. She was also named Director of the Performing Arts Training Center and the Dynamic Museum, with her offices and home located in the East St. Louis ghetto area among the people with whom she expected to work. The house assigned to her was at 532 North Tenth Street. The lower floor windows were boarded up. Across the street were other houses with burned-out interiors and shattered windows, among vacant lots where houses had been destroyed altogether in former upsurges of violence.

To start off the East St. Louis program, fifty young people at high school level were chosen as a pilot group. Divided into groups of ten, each group had a special counselor. College training was not considered important in the selection of these counselors. Instead they were picked for having backgrounds similar to the students, and hence greater understanding of them. Two counselors were graduates of a California rehabilitation program for former prison inmates. In working with their students, the counselors' aims were to help with "guidance, goal-seeking and self-realization."

Unable to personally reach all the young people she wished to enroll in the program, Katherine's plan was to teach the teachers who would then transmit attitudes and information to the students. The use of textbooks was minimized. Learning difficulties were tackled with teaching machines and programmed instruction.

"Some of the students are learning things they

never thought possible," Katherine reported a year
and a half after the project was under way. By that
time thirty-eight of their students were attending college on special scholarships at S.I.U.'s Edwardsville
campus or other universities. Only twelve people had
dropped out of the program.

Soon after the school started, the Dynamic Museum
opened as a glamorous teaching aid. Here were objects
from all over the world that the Dunham Dance
Company had picked up in their years of travel. John
Pratt, Katherine's husband, was curator of the museum, called "Dynamic" because things on display
could be touched and used. John's colorful costumes
were shown along with foreign theatre posters, programs, and books. There were records and films available showing the Katherine Dunham company in
action at the height of their fame. There were also
hats made of African cowrie shells, Haitian ceremonial drums, Ecuadorian head-dresses, Spanish sea
chests, Phillipine fiber slippers, and much more.

When the museum opened, a newspaper reporter
asked Katherine if she suffered any pangs of nostalgia
over seeing all these remembrances of things past. On
the contrary, she said, "I enjoy living with my mem-
orabilia which are probably the nearest thing to a
permanent home I have ever had." It was important,
she stressed, to "transmit the meaning and feel of the
objects to the people" so they would become more
personally aware of "the roots of the inheritance of
the American Negro and his biculture."

To Katherine the Dynamic Museum was visible

proof of the fact that, "I have explored all of the cultures of the dark-skinned people and it has made me wish that all ghetto-bred blacks could travel and see that we are a people belonging to a vast complex. We have status. All the Black power movement is a seeking for status."

Katherine's own status was now well recognized, not only by her own people. In 1968 she received the Professional Achievement Award from the University of Chicago Alumni Association honoring her for having brought distinction to herself in her vocational field as well as "credit to the University and real benefit to her fellow citizens."

During her East St. Louis residence, other awards were showered on Katherine. She won the Distinguished Service Award from Southern Illinois University, the Eight Lively Arts Award, and an award from the Black Academy of Arts and Letters. The framed citations hang in her office on North Tenth Street. Reflecting her wide range of interests and considerable achievements, the wall also holds certificates of membership in the Screen Actors' Guild, Actor's Equity, the American Society of Composers, Authors and Publishers, and the Royal Society of Anthropologists. There are acknowledgments for her services to the Hollywood Canteen during World War II, and for distinguished contributions to world poetry given by the International Who's Who in Poetry, along with the certificates of honor and merit that made her an officer in the Haitian Legion of Honor.

Dance Magazine in 1969 commended Katherine as "forerunner of the numerous fine contemporary Negro groups now emerging and developing . . . first of the fighters for the Negro dance company." Her friend, Dr. Erich Fromm, in presenting the award said, "An artist is always someone who is intensely alive and responsive to the human condition. Katherine Dunham is very much alive . . . She manages to retain her identity in the midst of change."

Applause is the recognition a trouper likes the most. Katherine continued to win it—for her dance training of young ghetto residents, and choreography for such shows as *Ode To Taylor Jones* and *Dream Deferred*, as well as for "Missa Luba," a Catholic mass set to Congolese folk tunes and performed during Negro History Week at St. Louis, Missouri, in February 1972.

Leading critics of the dance and theatre gave her high praise for her achievements. Writer and critic Arthur Todd believed that Katherine Dunham "put serious Negro dancing on the map once and for all." *New York Times* reviewer John Martin said she was a "superb performer and an illuminating personality." Dancer-choreographer Agnes de Mille stated that Katherine "pioneered in a difficult field, cutting away from all traditional clichés and presenting the Negro in fresh, astute and delicately observed moods." Dance critic Walter Terry thought Katherine Dunham "celebrated the strength, the fortitude, the faith, the prowess, and the majesty" of the black race. She was "a true original," added critic Clive Barnes.

Some of Katherine's former dance company members were still working with her in 1972, on *Treemonisha*, an opera by black composer Scott Joplin. Others were involved in the East St. Louis project despite past quarrels and conflicts. Through visits and correspondence, Katherine's old friendships in Europe, North and South America, Haiti, and Africa were kept alive. Loyalty was always a strong point in her character and foremost was loyalty to her own race. But her friends were black and white. She did not choose them, or her husband either, by the color of their skin.

Early in her career Katherine had said: "I would feel I'd failed miserably if I were doing dance confined to race, color or creed. I don't think that would be art, which has to do with universal truths." But what she has done, she said, "is broaden the horizon of the American Negro, showing both the unwilling people in America and outside of America the constructive potentialities of the Negro . . . I have provided careers and opportunities to many hundreds of young people. I believe that I can very well say that I am among the first, especially in the theatre, to make it a constructive thing to be a Negro, and to give him back his own cultural roots."

When *Treemonisha* was performed at Southern Illinois University's Carbondale campus in late 1972, Katherine got a standing ovation. It was apparent to anyone attending that show, that the audience was applauding not only the musicians and all black cast of singers and dancers, but also the talent and spirit of the entire black race as personified and given leadership by sixty-three-year-old Katherine Dunham, standing onstage to take a bow.

Katherine had once been asked what she would like to have inscribed on her tombstone. Her answer was, "She tried." The evidence is that she richly succeeded.

Terry Harnan graduated cum laude from Montclair State College. She was an assistant editor at *Look* Magazine, and later a reporter and then assistant editor at *Life* Magazine for sixteen years. While at *Life*, Terry Harnan worked on such noted series as "The World We Live In," "How the West Was Won," and "Miracle of Greece." Much of her work was in the youth and education departments.

Ms. Harnan is the author of *Gordon Parks, Black Photographer and Film Maker*, and two detective stories. She lives in Southold, New York, where she is a member of the Southold Town Conservation Advisory Commission.